VATICAN II — MARIAN COUNCIL

VATICAN II
MARIAN COUNCIL

By

WILLIAM G. MOST

PROFESSOR AT LORAS COLLEGE

 St Paul Publications

Nihil Obstat:

> ATTILIUS TEMPRA, S.S.P.
> Censor deputatus
> Die 3 Maii, 1972

Imprimatur:

> + **JOANNES McCORMACK**
> Epus. Midensis
> Datum apud Mullingar
> Die 23 Maii, 1972

Printed by:

ALBA HOUSE, ST. PAUL PUBLICATIONS, Athlone, Ireland

TABLE OF CONTENTS

TABLE OF CONTENTS

1 — UPGRADING THE DOWNGRADE

"Council votes to downgrade Mary." That is the way the headlines ran, one warm day in October, 1963, as a result of a heated day at the Council. Since that day, devotion to Mary, interest in the doctrine about her have declined sharply. More than one well-backed report is heard of priests trying to talk older people out of saying the Rosary, of nuns giving it up as out of date since Pope John.

What is the real truth about the Council action? In the interest of intellectual honesty, we ought to try to find out.

Our first clue comes from the actual records of the Council. The question had been raised: Should the Council speak of Mary in a separate document, or in the document on the Church?

The very strength of the feelings running at the Council made it advisable to find a way to avoid endless wrangling on the floor. It was agreed that each side should choose a spokesman to present its views.

First spoke Cardinal Santos, from the Philippines. He defended the use of a separate document for Mary, and in the course of his presentation, he endorsed some of the most advanced theological positions about her. For example: "She stood, suffering with Him as He died for us, meriting Redemption with Him."

Then Cardinal Koenig of Vienna arose to speak for the opposition. If anyone would favour "downgrading" it should be he, the champion of the forces opposed to the

Santos group. His very first words were these: "I do not contradict the things that are presented by the other eminent Father in this matter. I contradict neither as to the doctrine nor as to the devotion that flows from it. In fact, I very gladly and with my heart agree with all these things."

Cardinal Santos had defended a most advanced doctrine: that Mary shared in redeeming us. Cardinal Koenig, leader of the faction which the press said favoured downgrading, not only does not contradict: he heartily accepts and concurs.

What should one think of the integrity of a press that pretends to give the facts, actually gives the opposite!

We ought to explore the *real* teaching of the Council on Mary. For that purpose, we will trust no commentator, no supposed authority. We will work from the actual words of the Council itself. (To simplify references: All quotations from Vatican II in this chapter are taken from Chapter 8 of the Constitution on the Church, unless otherwise noted. We will, however, add, at suitable points, in the body of the text, the marginal numbers of the Council text).

To begin our survey of the teachings of the Council on Mary:

After describing her free acceptance of the role of Mother of God at the Annunciation, the Council adds (§ 56): "Rightly then do the Holy Fathers [of the Church] judge that Mary was not just employed by God in a passive way, but that she co-operated in human salvation by free faith and obedience. For she, as St. Irenaeus says, "being obedient, became a cause of salvation for herself and the whole human race."

Before going on to explore the remarkable implications of this statement, we might note in passing the stress the Council places on Mary's obedience, a hated word in our times. Many are saying: "If I do something because

I am commanded, there is little or no spiritual value in it." The Council not only disagrees, but teaches instead the opposite. The value of Mary's consent was precisely in her obedience. In fact, in the very first chapter of the same document, the Council makes our entire Redemption depend on obedience (§ 3): "By His obedience He (Christ) brought about Redemption."

The Council, as we saw, quoted St. Irenaeus, one of the early Fathers, who was Bishop of Lyons in Southern Gaul in the second century. His words are of special interest because he himself tells us that when he was young he had often listened to St. Polycarp, Bishop of Smyrna, recount what he had heard St. John the Apostle say, during the last years when John lived at Ephesus, near Smyrna.

If we read the full passage in St. Irenaeus, from which the Council quoted, we find that he was comparing and contrasting Mary with Eve. Eve, says St. Irenaeus, had contributed to bringing down upon us the ruin of sin. Mary contributed to undoing that evil. "Just as she [Eve] . . . being disobedient, became a cause of death for herself and the whole human race, so Mary . . . being obedient, became a cause of salvation for herself and the whole human race."

St. Irenaeus had also compared all sin, original and personal, to a tangled knot, and then added: ". . . for in no other way can that which is tied be untied unless the very windings of the knot are gone through in reverse . . . Thus, then, the knot of the disobedience of Eve was untied through the obedience of Mary."

He means this: If one wants to undo a tangled knot, he must take the end of the cord, make it go in reverse through every twist and turn that was made in tying it. Then and only then will the knot be untied.

Mary, says St. Irenaeus, untied what Eve had tied.

Now St. Irenaeus was commenting on the scene of the Annunciation, the day of the Incarnation, which began the process of Redemption. He says that Mary cooperated in redeeming us. Did he have in mind a cooperation by Mary that went beyond that day? We do not know. His knot comparison *should* imply more, for the knot was not really untied at the Annunciation: Calvary was needed to complete the work. So his words should imply that she shared in the Redemption not just by being the Mother of the Redeemer, the one from whom He received the flesh without which He, a Divine Person, could not have died. The comparison could mean that she took part in the great sacrifice itself.

Really, St. Irenaeus was an instrument in the hands of Divine Providence. He himself may not have seen all that the Spirit saw, and intended to begin to convey to the Church through his words. But St. Irenaeus was far from alone: this theme of the New Eve had appeared already in the Dialogue with Trypho of St. Justin, born in Palestine not long after 100 A.D. Christ, he says " . . . was made man of the Virgin, so that the disobedience brought on by the serpent might be cancelled out in the same manner in which it had begun . . . For Eve . . . brought forth disobedience and death. But Mary . . . answered: 'Be it done to me according to your word.' " We note again that St. Justin puts a stress on obedience.

Out of the many Fathers who give this same doctrine, we might listen to just one more. Tertullian, writing only slightly later, about 210 A.D. said: ". . . God, by a rival method, restored His image . . . For into Eve . . . had crept the word that established death; likewise, into a Virgin was to be brought the Word of God that produced life, so that what had gone to ruin by the one sex, might be restored to salvation by the same sex."

Even if we had only these three witnesses to Catholic teaching, we would be able to be sure that the New Eve parallel, with its important implication on the Redemption, was part of divine revelation. For Tertullian mirrors the faith of the Church in Africa; Irenaeus, the Church in Asia Minor and Gaul, and Justin, the Church in Palestine. Thus between them they can reflect the fact that the entire Church believed in the New Eve, and had begun to understand that just as Eve contributed to the ruin of our race in original sin, so did Mary contribute to lifting that bane, by her obedience, joined to that of the New Adam.

Vatican II tells us the special force of something that is believed by the entire Church. In § 12 of the Constitution on the Church the Council says: "The entire body of the faithful, since it has the anointing from the Holy One, cannot be deceived in its belief." In other words, what the whole Church believes is infallible, even if the authorities of the Church have not yet issued a definition of that belief.

"She became a cause of salvation for herself and the whole human race." [1] Really, that is almost a shocking statement. Could a mere creature do that much? Could a being made out of nothing actually contribute to moving the Father to grant forgiveness and grace? Once we begin to realize the implications of saying that Mary shared in redeeming us, we are quite naturally inclined to say: of course it cannot really mean that. There must be some exaggeration. Probably it is just a bit of rhetorical praise.

Yet, St. Irenaeus did say that she "became a cause of salvation for herself and the whole human race." And, what is far more important, not only do the other Fathers of the Church, [2] with virtual unanimity, concur, but Vatican II quotes these words of St. Irenaeus for us, with obvious approval.

Now of course, St. Irenaeus, if we read the full passage, clearly had in mind the scene of the Annunciation. Seen in that context, his words could mean merely that by providing the Divine Redeemer with the flesh without which He could not have died, she did contribute to our salvation. That, of course, would obviously be a real co-operation in the work of salvation. She certainly did that. Yet, as we saw, St. Irenaeus compared Redemption to the untying of a tangled knot, the knot of sin, and Mary shared in that work of untying the knot. Now, as we know, the knot was not undone at the Annunciation: that work called for the great sacrifice itself. So, did she really have something to contribute there too? We need to press further in our study of the teaching of Vatican II on this point.

Shortly after the statement we have already seen from the Council, in the very next paragraph, we find this:[3] "This union of the Mother with the Son in the work of salvation, is evident, from the time of the virginal conception of Christ, even to His death."

This is a sweeping statement. It not only asserts she was joined with Him in the work of salvation: it adds that this union was continuous, and that it lasted "even to His death." This could hardly mean anything other than that she *did* share in the work of Redemption even on Calvary. But there is more.

In the very next paragraph the Council becomes more explicit:[4] "In faith she bore with her union with her Son"; of course, she by no means wanted anything other than to be united with him. Yet, to be joined to a suffering Messiah is to be pierced with a sword, as Simeon had prophesied. Hence the Council said she "bore with" or endured this union. But to complete the text: "In faith she bore with her union with her Son, even to the cross, where she stood, in accord with the divine plan, greatly grieved with her Only-begotten, and joined herself to His sacrifice with a Motherly heart, consenting to the immolation of the victim that had been born of her." We can see now why the Council used that word that at first sounded so strange, "she *bore with* her union." We can also begin to see in what her role on Calvary consisted: it was one of suffering with him, one of joining herself to His sacrifice, one of consenting that the Victim, who was her Son, be immolated.

Rightly could she have cried out that it was all the most incredible outrage: that Innocence itself should be condemned, that the giver of life should die, that He who was precisely then taking away the guilt of the world should be

15

shamed as if guilty Himself. But she knew that such was His will, such was the will of the Father. At the Annunciation, she had willingly said: *Fiat:* be it done to me according to your word. Now she would not take it back, she would live out, bitterly, the last dread implication of those words.

A bit farther on, in a section dealing with the relation of Our Lady to the Church, of which she is the model or type, the Council adds a further precision to what it had already said: [5] "In conceiving Christ, in bringing Him forth, in nourishing Him, in presenting Him to the Father in the Temple, in suffering with her Son as He died on the Cross, she cooperated in the work of the Saviour in an altogether singular way, by obedience, faith, hope, and burning love, to restore supernatural life to souls. As a result, she is our mother in the order of grace."

Rich is the content of this Conciliar teaching. We note first that she cooperated precisely in the heart of the Redemption itself, that is, "she cooperated in the work of the Saviour" which was "to restore supernatural life to souls." But further, and this is very important; the Council says that she cooperated in the work of the Saviour "in an altogether singular way." Why say her cooperation was altogether singular? Because for long we have been taught that each of us cooperates in his own salvation, by working with grace. In fact, Pope Pius XI, in an exhortation to young people engaged in Catholic Action, urged them to become [6] "co-redeemers." But the Council wanted to say that, legitimate as these expressions are, it meant something quite different when it spoke of Mary's cooperation in the Redemption. Therefore it called her role "altogether singular", that is, one quite different from the cooperation of all others.

How was her role singular? We might say there are

two phases to the work of Redemption. The first, which is often called the objective Redemption, consists in the acquisition or earning of the inexhaustible treasury of forgiveness and grace for all men; the second, called subjective Redemption, is the application of those graces to men in all times, the giving out of the riches of the once-for-all acquired treasury. Mary, sharing as she did even on Calvary, had a part even in the once-for-all acquisition of the great treasury.

In just *what way* did she cooperate? The Council says it was "by obedience, faith, hope, and burning love." Actually, as we will see later on, these four almost merge into one thing. But for now we want to focus our attention on the fact that an essential part, the very heart of her cooperation was her obedience. We noted in our first chapter that the Council began its teaching on Mary's cooperation by speaking of her obedience. It had said still earlier of her Son that [7] "by His obedience He brought about Redemption." Now, in explaining the *how* of her cooperation in redeeming us, the Council again stresses obedience. Obedience is hardly a popular topic today. It is something that even the best of Catholics do not find easy or to their liking. Yet it was an essential means of Redemption itself. At the Annunciation Mary had obeyed, willingly saying her *Fiat*. That *Fiat* had, according to the Epistle to the Hebrews, been really an echo of the first reaction of the heart of the Incarnate Christ: [8] "On entering into the world he said: A sacrifice and offering you did not wish, but you provided a body for me. You did not take pleasure in holocausts for sins. Then I said: Behold, I come. At the head of the book it is written concerning me: I come to do your will, O God." Both He and she had pledged obedience at the outset. Now both were carrying it out: He in His own blood, being obedient even to death, [9] even to death on a cross; she, as the Council said "consenting to the immolation of the victim that had been born of her."

St. Paul wrote to the Romans: [10] "Just as by the disobedience of the one man", the old Adam, "the many", a Hebraism [11] for the numerous *all*, "were made sinners, so by the obedience of the one man", the New Adam, "the many will be made just." St. Irenaeus completed the canvas begun by St. Paul. Just as there was a New Adam to undo the disobedience of the Old Adam, so too there was a New Eve: [12] "Just as she . . . being disobedient, became a cause of death for herself and the whole human race, so Mary . . . being obedient, became a cause of salvation for herself and the whole human race."

Who now will dare to say: "If I do it because I am told, it is no good?" Who will be even bolder, and attribute his error to Vatican II?

St. Pius X had written of Mary: [13] " . . . since . . . she was associated by Christ with Himself in the work of human redemption, she merited for us congruously, as they say, what Christ merited condignly . . . " Pope Benedict XV had added: [14] "With her suffering and dying Son, Mary endured suffering and almost death. She gave up her Mother's rights over her Son to procure the salvation of mankind, and, to appease the divine justice, she, as much as she could, immolated her Son, so that one can truly affirm that together with Christ she has redeemed the human race." The great Pope of Mary, Pius XII had said: [15] "She it was who, free from all sin, original and personal, and always most intimately united with her Son, as the New Eve, offered Him on Golgotha, together with the holocaust of her maternal rights and love . . ." Vatican II went precisely as far as the great Popes of the past, even as far as the great Pius XII in its Marian doctrine. Both the Popes and the Council taught that she shared in redeeming us, not only by being the Mother of the Redeemer, but even by her altogether singular cooperation in the great sacrifice itself, on Calvary.

What irony! What a reversal and perversion of the truth! Vatican II went farther than any Council in the entire history of the Church in its Marian teachings. It even equalled the great Marian Pope Pius XII in its teaching on her. Yet some have dared to assert that Vatican II gave the signal for downgrading Mary. In fact, one noted ecumenist, who was present at the Council — we will withhold his name, out of charity — dared to write in March, 1964, *after* the Council had drafted the chapter from which we have quoted: [16] "... the two doctrinal positions of Mary's co-redemption and her universal mediation ... have ... largely lost their relevance ... If ... the redemptive sacrifice ... includes His resurrection ... then the question of any other person sharing in its execution does not really make sense."

Really, even if Vatican II had not written so much as one line of the passages we have quoted, it still reaffirmed the Marian teaching of the previous Popes by just one sweeping statement, found in § 25 of the same document, the Constitution on the Church: "... religious submission of will and of mind must be shown in a special way to the authentic Magisterium of the Roman pontiff even when he is not speaking ex cathedra [defining] that is [it must be shown] in such a way that ... the statements pronounced by him are sincerely adhered to."

So there is really no need to ask whether or not we can still hold to the great teachings of previous Popes on Mary. We not only *may*. Vatican II says we *must*. In fact, if any Council in all the centuries of the Church deserves the title, Vatican II could be rightly called: The Marian Council. No other Council went so far, spoke so extensively of her as it did.

1. Vatican II, On the Church § 56.

2. E.g., St. Justin Martyr, **Dialog with Trypho,** 100; Tertullian, **On the Flesh of Christ,** 17; St. Cyril of Jerusalem, **Catechesis** 12,15; St. Jerome, **Epist.** 22,21; St. Ambrose, **On the Gospel of Luke,** 4,7; St. Augustine, **On the Christian Combat** 22,24.

3. On the Church § 57.

4. **Ibid.,** § 58.

5. **Ibid.,** § 61

6. Cited from J.B. Carol, O.F.M., **De Corredemptione** (Vatican City, 1950) p. 529.

7. On the·Church § 3.

8. Heb. 10,5-7.

9. Phil. 2,8.

10. Rom. 5,19.

11. Cf. a similar use of "many" in Is. 53,12 and the explicit recognition by Vatican II (On Missions § 3): "The Son of Man did not come to be ministered to but to minister and to give His life as a redemption for many, that is, for all".

12. St. Irenaeus, **Against Heresies,** 3,22,4, quoted by Vatican II in, On the Church § 56.

13. St. Pius X, **Ad diem illum,** Feb. 2, 1904: ASS 36,454.

14. Benedict XV, **Inter Sodalicia,** May 22, 1918: AAS 10,182.

15. Pius XII, **Mystici Corporis,** June 29, 1943: AAS 35,247.

16. The Constitution on the Church was not formally promulgated until Nov. 21, 1964, but the writer in question was at the Council while it was being drafted.

3 — YOU WERE BOUGHT AT A PRICE

St. Paul speaks more than once of a price of Redemption: [1] "You were bought at a price." Now, since we know from the teachings of Vatican II that Mary cooperated in that Redemption, we naturally need to ask: What is her relation to the "price of Redemption"? Did she actually contribute to paying it? At once we see an immense problem: How could any mere creature, however exalted, share in moving the Father to grant forgiveness and grace? But yet: If she did not share in paying that price, what could it mean to say she shared in the Redemption on Calvary?

Long before the Council, these questions were under hot discussion by many theological specialists. Opinions were sharply divided. At the start of Chapter 8, in which the chief Marian teaching of the Council is given, we find this statement [2] "...it does not have in mind to present a complete doctrine about Mary, nor to settle questions not yet brought into full light by the labour of theologians." So, we must not expect to find the answer to our question in Vatican II. But that does not mean we may not try to find it, with the help of further theological study, and also with the help of certain *implications* in official teachings.

Before taking up the question of Mary's possible contribution to the price, we need to look at two preliminary but basic questions, namely: To whom was the price paid? Did the price really *move* the Father?

When we ask to whom the price was paid, we seem

at once to be faced with a dilemma. If we say the price was paid to the Father, the problem is twofold. First, the Father was not the one who, as it were, held the human race captive. But ransom or a price is paid to the captor. Second, even if He were, as St. Gregory Nazianzus said: [3] "Why would the blood of His Only-begotten please the Father." That is: The Father would hardly take pleasure in seeing His only Son die.

But then, should we say the price was paid to the devil? For the devil was, as it were the captor, who held our race in his power. A few of the early Fathers of the Church actually did consider this possibility seriously. Even the soberly Roman St. Ambrose was willing to write: [4] "Without doubt he [the devil] demanded a price to set free from slavery those whom he held bound. Now the price of our liberty was the blood of Jesus, which necessarily had to be paid to him to whom we were sold by our sins."

However, most of the Fathers either passed such a possibility by in eloquent silence, or explicitly rejected it.

Of course, there is no other person who might even possibly be considered as receiving the price.

So, if it is not the Father, and surely not the devil, what should we say? That there is no price at all? But the inspired words of St. Paul tell us there was such a price.

The real answer seems to be found in a little noticed bit of theology, that is both new and old [5] from Pope Paul VI. In the doctrinal introduction to his decree on indulgences, given in January 1967, he wrote: [6] "As we are taught by divine revelation, punishments inflicted by divine holiness and justice follow upon sins ... These penalties are imposed by the merciful judgment of God to purify souls *and to defend the sanctity of the moral order,* and to restore the glory of God to its full majesty. For *every sin brings with it a disturbance of the universal order,* which God

arranged in His inexpressible wisdom and infinite love . . .
So, *it is necessary for the full remission and reparation of
sins* . . . not only that friendship with God be restored . . .
but also that all the goods, both individual and social, *and
those that belong to the universal order, which were less-
ened or destroyed by sin, be fully reestablished, either through
voluntary reparation . . . or through suffering penalties* set by
the just and most holy wisdom of God." The Holy Father
put the Redemption within this framework, for he said there
is [7] "a treasury of the Church . . . which is the infinite and
inexhaustible price that the expiations and merits of Christ
have before God, offered that all humanity might be liberated from sin . . . "

Here at last is the solution that had evaded the in-
genuity of the early Fathers! There really is a price. It is not
paid to the Father, and of course, not to the devil. Rather,
it consists in this: Every sin damages the moral order. The
sinner, as it were, takes for himself more than he should.
God in His wisdom and justice [8] and love wants that order
maintained. Therefore, He wants it balanced again. How is
that done? Either the sinner himself will balance it, by giving up something he could have otherwise lawfully had,
or, someone else must do it for him. Christ, by His death,
balanced the scales for all sins. So the price was paid to
the moral order. Christ by His dread death put back into
the scales more than the excess taken from the moral order
by all sins of all time.

We begin to see another problem: If Christ paid our
debt so fully, even infinitely: Where could there possibly
be room for any contribution from Mary or any creature?
We need to face this problem. But before we can hope to
deal with it satisfactorily, we need to lay a groundwork,
by taking up the other question we raised early in this
chapter, namely: Did the price really *move* the Father?

Now if the price *moved* the Father, it would have to move Him to take some attitude or to do something. What would that be? It seems it would have to move Him to love mankind again, after being angry, and to grant forgiveness. Now, and this is most important, did the Father really have to be moved to love us again? St. John, the beloved Apostle, understood the matter well. He wrote: [9] "God so loved the world that He gave His Only-begotten Son." So, God loved men *before* the price was paid. Really, that is how the price came to be paid. It was because the Father always loved us that He sent His Son. Or, to put it another way: *The Father did not begin to love us because Christ came; rather, Christ came because the Father always loved us, even when we were in sin.*

We reach, then, this surprising result: Even the infinite offering of Christ did not move the Father. Why? He did not have to be moved to love us. He always did love us.

So then: What function can the price of Redemption have, if it did not move the Father? The key is found in the new theological development given us by Pope Paul VI, which we saw above. The Father wanted the price paid, not so He Himself would be moved, there was no need of that, but he wanted it paid out of His love for the moral order.

Now, a price that serves simply to restore the moral order is quite different from a price that would need to move the Infinite (which really could not be done anyway, for God is immutable).

We see then, that the problem of how Mary could possibly share in moving the Father does not exist: He was not moved even by the offering of His Son. He did not need to be moved. The price served to balance the unbalanced moral order. Mary could contribute to doing that. Any creature can, by penance, help put back what was wrongly taken.

But we still need to face the problem we postponed earlier: The reparation made by Christ is infinite. How then is there any room for her, or any creature, to contribute?

We can approach the problem by noticing that there were, humanly speaking, several ways in which the Father could have provided for Redemption. Once He decided to forgive sin, He could have done one of several things.

First, He could have simply forgiven the sin of our first parents, and resolved to forgive subsequent sins, without any reparation at all. Being absolute Master, that was within His rights. He chose not to do it that way, out of His love for moral goodness, for the moral order, and out of His love for us: He wanted to do more for us than that.

Second, He could have provided for a finite, but real, Redemption by appointing some mere human being to carry out any religious act, perhaps an Old Testament type sacrifice. He could even bind Himself by promise to accept it. He could, as it were, say: "Now this reparation is not equal to the damage of sin. Yet, creatures are not capable of full reparation. Therefore, I have decided to accept what they can do. This will be Redemption."

Third, He could have arranged for an infinite reparation in a much easier way than that which He actually took. He could have sent His Son to be born, not in the stable, but in a palace. He could have fitted out that palace with every luxury that the most advanced final science of the last century of the world could provide. And that Son would not have to die. On some set day, with representatives of the whole human race looking on in admiration, He would redeem the world. To do that, He would need only to say a short prayer, such as: "Father, forgive them." Then, without dying, He would ascend in a blaze of glory. That three word prayer, coming from an Infinite Person, would have infinite worth. It would be able to most fully redeem countless worlds.

But now we can see something astounding: *The Father literally went beyond the infinite,* for Redemption by a three word prayer would have been infinite. But the Father knew that still more *could be done.* Since His generosity was infinite, or rather, since He *is* infinite generosity, He would not be content with less if more could be provided. So He sent His Son, not to the palace but to the stable; not to redeem by an easy prayer without dying, but to become obedient even to the death of the cross.

In mathematics, infinity plus any conceivable addition does not grow. But we are not now in the terrain of mathematics: we are in the realm of divine generosity, which knows no limit.

So there is room for Mary in such a framework. For we have seen that the Father seems to have made this His principle: "I will not be content with less if more can be done." More could be done: hence He went beyond infinite Redemption by a mere prayer to a Redemption by the cross. Still more could be done: He could add the obedience of the New Eve to that of the New Adam. Or, since she was then the Church (the Apostles had fled) and the type [10] of the Church, as Vatican II says, the great price of Redemption could be the offering of the Whole Christ, [11] Head and Members.

The Vatican Council says that the Mass is the renewal [12] of the New Convenant. Now in the renewal, there is, all readily admit it, a twofold offering, the offering of Christ the Head, to which is joined the offering of His members, which we are. We really do join with Him in the offering of the Mass. So then, if the *renewal* is twofold, formed of the obedience of Christ to which is added that of His members, then would it not be strange if the *original,* which the renewal repeats, did not have a similar twofold structure? Really if the renewal were twofold, and the original not, then the renewal would be partly false, it would not repeat fully what it should repeat. Therefore, the original must have been twofold: Mary's offering, her obedience, must have fused as it were, with the obedient offering of Christ. His obedience, as we saw was the price of Redemption. Her obedience, said Vatican II, was joined with His. What else should that mean, if not that she shared in paying the very price [13] of Redemption!

We recall too, that as we saw, in thinking out the several ways in which the Father could have restored us, that He could have accepted any religious act of a mere creature as the *entire* Redemption (finite, but real). Obviously then, He could accept the great offering of the highest of mere creatures as *part* of the price of Redemption.

But when we say her contribution formed part of the price of Redemption we must not think of the cooperation of Jesus and Mary after the pattern of a team of two, pulling a load together. It would not even be accurate to think of it as of a team with two partners of unequal strength. For here, one member of the team not only has less strength, but all the strength she has comes from her partner and Master. She really does have power, she is not a non-entity, nor does she accomplish nothing, her offering is of real value, as we have said. But the correct image is to think of both Son and Mother as working together *as a unit* in which each accomplishes all with the other, even though the basis of the strength of the two is so very different; He is the source of both His own and her power. Without Him, she could do nothing. But like St. Paul she could still say: [14] "I can do all things in Him who strengthens me," even cooperate in redeeming the world.

And all this, if one cares to meditate further upon it, suggests still another most remarkable possibility about her relation to the Mass even today. But we must reserve that for a later chapter [15].

NOTES

1. 1 Cor. 6,20; 7,23.

2. On the Church § 54.

3. St. Gregory Nazianzus, Oration 45, on Easter, 22.

4. St. Ambrose, Epistle 72.

5. Scholastic theologians had long held this notion. It was also commonly taught by early Jewish rabbis. Cf. also St. Paul, Col. 1,24.

6. Paul VI, **Indulgentiarum doctrina,** Jan. 9, 1967: AAS 59,5-7.

7. **Ibid.,** 11-12.

8. Cf. Ps. 11,7: "The Lord is righteous, and He loves righteous things."

9. Jn. 3,16.

10. Cf. On the Church §§ 63-65.

11. Some modern authors think St. Paul speaks of a body of Christ, and of Christ the Head, but refuse to see that the two notions are combined in his thought to form the whole Christ. However, Pius XII beyond doubt did teach the full concept in his **Mystici Corporis** Encyclical, esp.: "We speak of Christ, Head and Body, the Whole Christ" (AAS 35,230).

12. On the Liturgy § 10.

13. We will see further evidence in Chapter 5.

14. Phil. 4,13.

15. Cf. Chapter 19.

4 — MOTHER OF ALL MEN

What a difference a few short words can make. "I do," can change a pair of lives. Mary's "be it done to me," started the process of Redemption. The Council too made a great difference in its Marian teaching by one short three word phrase, "as a result."

Had the Council said simply: "She is our Mother in the order of grace," that would have been the expression of an important, though well known truth. But the Council actually said: "As a result she is our Mother in the order of grace." As a result of what? The Council had just explained, as we saw in the last two chapters, that she shared in an altogether singular way by her obedience and love in the work of restoring supernatural life to souls, that is, in the Redemption itself. In fact, if our deductions in the last chapter are correct, it implies that she shared in the very price of Redemption itself. But whatever be the truth about her relation to the price of Redemption, there is no doubt that the Council did say this: She shared in the work of restoring supernatural life to souls and "as a result, she is our Mother in the order of grace."

In saying that her spiritual motherhood is the *result* of her cooperation in the Redemption, the Council opens up a rich spiritual perspective. We can approach it by looking at the function of a Mother in the merely natural order of things. A merely human Mother has two functions. First, she shares in bringing a new life into being; then, she takes care of that life, so long as there is need, and so long as she is able.

Now our bodily life is important, even most basic. Yet, in comparison to the life of the soul by which as the second Epistle of Peter says, we are made, [1] "sharers in the divine nature," what is that bodily life? St. Paul, who had been given a glimpse of the third heaven, [2] exclaims loudly that for the sake of Christ, by whom we share in that divinity, [3] "I have taken the loss of all things, and I consider them dung that I may gain Christ and may be found in Him." In comparison to such a divine life, our earthly life seems more like death than life. Now it is precisely that divine life that Mary shared in gaining for us at the Cross. at the cost of immense grief and pain to herself and her Divine Son. No wonder the Council proclaims that "as a result, she is our Mother in the order of grace." For truly she has brought us forth amid terrible birth pains, at the foot of the cross. It is not just in some figurative or metaphorical sense, but in the most real and literal sense, far more than our earthly Mothers, that she deserves the title of our Mother.

A Mother, as we said, should also take care of the new life so long as there is need, so long as she is able. In the natural order, children ordinarily reach a point at which they have no real need of further aid from their earthly Mother. But in the order of grace in which, as her Divine Son said: [4] "without me you can do nothing," in that realm, one never grows so great, matures so fully, as not to have need of the inflow of divine power. So our need of the grace that our Mother of grace brings us never comes to an end, not even if we come to be the [5] "perfect man, to the measure of the stature of the fulness of Christ." For even then it will still be true that through grace, [6] "it is God who works in you both the will and the doing."

A Mother in the ordinary human order does not always live long enough, or even if she lives, she may not be able to help the various needs of her offspring. But our Mother in heaven lives the unending life of eternity, and she is, moreover, able to ask any grace for us with the assurance that it will be given, for she shared in earning all graces for us at the moment of the great sacrifice. This is true precisely because that Sacrifice did earn all graces, and she shared in it, in that which earned not just some, but *all* graces. So no grace is beyond that which she may rightfully claim for us.

With such a concept in mind the Council wrote beautifully (§ 62): "This motherhood of Mary in the economy of grace continues unceasingly, from the consent which she gave in faith at the Annunciation, and which she unhesitatingly endured under the Cross, even until the eternal consummation of all the elect. For after she was assumed into heaven, she did not lay aside this role, but by her manifold intercession continues, winning the gifts [that is, graces] of eternal salvation by her intercession. By her Motherly love, she takes care of the brothers of her Son who are still on the way [to their eternal home] and who are involved in dangers and difficulties, until they are led to the blessed fatherland. For this reason the Blessed Virgin is invoked in the Church with the titles of Advocate, Auxiliatrix, Helper, and Mediatrix."

The Council notes wisely that her motherhood over us really began on the day of the Annunciation, with the conception of Christ. And obviously. For by the very fact that she became the Mother of Christ the Head, she necessarily became at the same time the Mother of the Members of the Whole Christ. Hence the Council speaks of us as the "brothers of her Son," for in conceiving Him physically, she could not do other than also conceive us spiritually at the same time. She began then the process of winning the life of heaven, divine life, for us. That role led her to "endure" the effects of her consent at the Cross. For the *Fiat* she pronounced when the angel came to her, necessarily committed her to her role on Calvary. And this Motherhood, the Council notes, did not cease when she left this earth. Rather, she continues to exercise her care over us even in heaven, by caring for us who are still in dangers, who have not yet reached the blessed Fatherland. "For this reason," adds the Council, she is invoked under "the titles of Advocate, Auxiliatrix, Helper, and Mediatrix."

The Council did not add the words "of all graces" to the title of Mediatrix. Yet that truth is evident in more than one way.

First of all, as we have already noticed, she shared in the great Sacrifice which actually won all graces. Since she shared in earning *all* graces, certainly in that sense, all are given through her Motherly influence. Pope Paul VI, in his constitution *Indulgentiarum doctrina* tells us that the Saints, being [7] "present before God . . . do not cease to intercede with the Father, presenting the merits which they gained on earth." That expression "presenting the merits" is, clearly, a figure of speech. It does not mean that in any literal sense they hold up a paten before the face of God, on which are placed their merits. Rather, it means that the force of their prayers rests chiefly on the fact that by their merits on this earth they earned the graces for which they ask. Now Mary, as we have said, shared in the Sacrifice that earned not just some, but *all* graces. So the merits she "presents" to the Father, do apply to all graces. Obviously then, in at least this sense, she is the Mediatrix of all, not just of some graces.

Further, since she has been divinely assigned the role of Spiritual Mother, it is part of her Motherly function to care for all the needs of her children.

It is not too much to suppose she could know of and

ask for all of our spiritual needs. For, on the one hand, the very fact that she was divinely commissioned to the role of Mother of all means that she should be divinely enabled to know what she needs to know in order to carry out that role. Further, any Saint whatsoever is able to see, in the infinite vision in which all knowledge is contained, all that pertains to him. But to her, as Mother of all, do pertain the needs of all. So again, she must be able to see all our needs.

But we need not rely just on our own deductions to determine that she is the Mediatrix of *all* graces. For, as we saw in chapter 2 the Council reaffirmed in a block all previous papal teachings, on Marian as well as other doctrinal matters. Still further, the Council itself added a footnote to the sentence in which it called her Mediatrix. The note sends us to statements of several Popes. We shall examine just two of them.

Speaking of the intensification of her role of intercession after the Assumption, Pope Leo XIII says: [8] "For thereupon, in accord with the divine plan, she began so to watch over the Church, so to be with us and cherish us as Mother that she who had been the helper in the accomplishment of the mystery of human Redemption, should also be the helper in the distribution of the grace coming from it for all time, *practically measureless* power being given to her."

We note that the Pope distinguishes the two phases of the Redemption which we spoke above in chapter 2, that is, the objective Redemption, which is, briefly, the *earning* of the inexhaustible treasury of forgiveness and grace for men on Calvary, and the subjective Redemption, which is the giving out of that same treasury. Pope Leo brings the two phrases into parallel: just as she shared in earning grace, so, naturally, she shares in giving it out. But, as we noted above, that objective Redemption, the great Sacrifice, earned *all* graces, not just some. Hence, since her role is, according to the Pope, parallel in the two phases, she should share in dispensing *all*. He seems to further suggest the same conclusion at the end of the passage by adding that "practically measureless power" is given to her. That word "measureless" could refer to the question of *what kind* of graces she could obtain for us: seen under that aspect, it would mean that she can obtain any kind of grace, that nothing is too great. But "measureless" can obviously also imply another aspect, not now the *kind,* but the *number* of graces, i.e., does she intervene in the giving out of *all* graces? The words of Pope Leo are not so clear as to exclude all possibility of a different interpretation: yet they at least seem to imply that her mediation extends to *all* graces.

Any lingering doubt we might feel after reading the teaching of Pope Leo XIII vanishes completely when we turn to the second of the texts to which the Council refers us, the *Ad diem illum* of Pope St. Pius X. He wrote this Encyclical to solemnly commemorate the 50th anniversary of the definition of the dogma of the Immaculate Conception. After describing the terrible sorrows of Mary with her Son beneath the Cross, the Holy Pontiff continues: [9] "Now from this common sharing of will and suffering between Christ and Mary, she 'merited to become most worthily the Reparatrix of the lost world,' and therefore, Dispensatrix of *all* the gifts which Jesus gained for us by His death and His blood."

Pope St. Pius X, like his predecessor, brings out the parallel, that since she had shared in earning grace, she similarly shared in dispensing it. But we notice that he states most plainly that she is Dispensatrix not just of some, but of all [10] graces.

When we were small children in the merely human

order, we tended to think our parents could do practically anything. Later we had to learn that they had their limitations. But in the order of grace, thanks to the goodness of our Father in heaven, we have a Mother whose power to help us is without limit.

Her Divine Son told us: [11] "Amen I say to you, if you do not change and become as children, you will not get into the kingdom of heaven." He was speaking to an audience of those who were physically adults. He meant all of us as well. He wanted us to know that when and if we finally do reach the mansions of the Father in Heaven, the *basic* reason will be, not our merit, but the goodness and generous gift of our Father in Heaven, given us through our spiritual Mother. In the natural order, children receive the love and care of their parents, not because they, the children, are good or earn that love and care. Really, it is too great for them to earn, they could not possibly merit it. But they do not have to earn it: it is given them not because they, the children, are good, but because the parents are good, are lovingly generous.

So too it is in the order of grace. We do, of course merit, and God does reward and punish justly. But that merit of ours is not the *basic* reason why we are given divine grace in the first place, and finally, heaven itself. The basic reason is unmerited grace. We might put it this way: Grace (sanctifying grace) is as it were our *title,* (we might almost compare it to a ticket), to enter our Father's house. The basic, the first gift of that grace, as St. Paul [12] insists over and over again, is given us with no merit of ours. Really, our very ability to merit depends on our being sons of God. But that status of sons of God is obtained precisely by the first [13] gift of sanctifying grace. Obviously, then, we cannot merit the very basis on which we merit. It would be like trying to lift ourselves off the floor by pulling up on our shoelaces.

We see, then, that this teaching of the spiritual Motherhood of Mary is more than just a pleasant, consoling thought. It teaches us how to take the correct, the indispensable attitude to our Father in Heaven, the attitude without which "you will not get into the kingdom of heaven."

Still further, this doctrine helps us to see something that would otherwise be difficult to come to know. We have been told that God is our Father. We tend to think of a Father as one who is loving, but also just, who will punish when that is called for. We tend to think of a Mother as one who is also loving and just, but with this difference: she is, we feel, specially inclined to hold off from punishing, to use painful measures only as a last resort.

Now if we had read that God is our Mother [14] as well as our Father, it would have been likely to confuse us. Yet, His love for us does have that motherly quality of persistence, of being unwilling to resort to stern measures if they can be avoided. For that reason our Master Himself as He wept over the hardness of Jerusalem, exclaimed: "How often have I wanted to gather together your children, as a hen [15] does her chicks, but you were not willing."

But Divine Wisdom found a means of bringing out both aspects of the truth clearly and without confusion. For we are taught that we have not only a good Father in heaven, but also a Mother, who shared in bringing us to the divine life of grace, who takes care of us with a power that is practically speaking limitless, in giving out to us, her children all the graces we ever receive, since she shared, at such dread cost, in earning all of them for us.

The thoughts we have just dwelt on consider her as the Mother of each individual man. We should add that Pope Paul VI, at the closing of the third session of the Council, also proclaimed her as "Mother of the Church." The reasoning is obvious. As we said above, she, being the Mother of Christ the Head, is, automatically, by that very fact, the Mother of the Members of Christ. This is true not only of them individually: the Mother of the Head must be the Mother of the Body. But that Body, the Mystical Body of Christ, *is* the Church. Vatican II itself said it explicitly, echoing St. Paul: [16] "He is the Head of the Body, which is the Church." 	,

Really, then, the declaration of Pope Paul VI was not something new: it was bringing out that which was very evidently implied in the teaching of the Council itself [17].

NOTES

1. 2 Pet. 1,4.

2. 2 Cor. 12,2.

3. Phil. 3,8-9.

4. Jn. 15,5.

5. Eph. 4,13.

6. Phil. 2,13.

7. AAS 59,12; Cf. W. Most, "The Nature of Mary's Intercession: Its Scriptural Basis" in: **Marian Studies**, 22 (1971) 27-48.

8. Leo XIII, **Adiutricem populi**, Sept. 5, 1895; ASS 28,130 (in the Council reference to this document there is a misprint in the number). For "practically measureless" the Latin has: **paene immensa.**

9. St. Pius X, **Ad diem illum**: ASS 36,453-54 (citing Eadmer). Italics added.

10. Some Mariologists think we may say Mary intervenes in the dispensation of all graces not only in that she earned all, and that her **intercession** is at work in dispensing all, but also that she is as

it were a physical **instrument** of their transmission. The theory is plausible, but not proved.

11. Mt. 18,3.

12. We cannot earn the first gift of grace, which is, as it were, the ticket to heaven. So salvation itself is unearned, in its **basic** degree. Yet, on a secondary level, we do earn. And, even though we do not earn on the primary level, we can earn to be deprived of it. Cf. W. Most, "A Biblical Theory of Redemption in a Covenant Framework" in: **Catholic Biblical Quarterly**, Jan. 1967, esp. pp. 12-14.

13. By "first gift" we mean not only its first reception in Baptism, but also its recovery after falling into the state of sin.

14. Cf. Mt. 23,37; Ps. 27,10; Is. 49,15.

15. St. Augustine makes the apt observation that the hen is the most obviously motherly of animals: **Tracts on St. John's Gospel**, 15,7.

16. On the Church § 7; Cf. Col. 1, 18.

17. Actually, the title had been used by several Popes before him, beginning with Gregory XVI. E.g., Leo XIII, in his **Adiutricem populi** (ASS 28,130) said she was "most truly the Mother of the Church." Cf. G.M. Roschini, "Mother of the Church" in: **Our Lady's Digest** 19 (1965) 270-77, and George Shea, "Pope Paul VI and the 'Mother of the Church'" in: **Marian Studies** 16 (1965) 21-28.

5 — I DESIRE TO BE DISSOLVED ...

What was the life of our Blessed Mother like from the time her Son left this earth until her own Assumption? Scripture gives us only two scant indications. At the foot of the Cross, the beloved disciple John heard: [1] "Behold your Mother. And from that hour the disciple took here to his home." Vatican II, quoting from Acts of the Apostles, says that [2] "before the day of Pentecost, we see the Apostles 'persevering with one heart in prayer with the women and with Mary the Mother of Jesus and His brothers,' and Mary too with her prayers imploring the gift of the Spirit, who already at the Annunciation had overshadowed her." Of course, we may assume that she went with St. John to Ephesus some time after that first Pentecost. But beyond that, we know nothing, except that she was assumed into heaven.

We do not even know for certain that she died at all. We are much inclined to assume that she did, as a matter of likeness to her Divine Son. But we are not certain. St. John Damascene puts it well: [3] "How could she, from whom flowed forth true Life, taste death? But she yielded to the law made by Him whom she begot, and ... underwent the ancient sentence, for even her Son, who is Life itself, did not refuse it." Actually, a few Fathers, St. Epiphanius and St. Ambrose, [4] make vague statements which some have taken as implying a denial that she died. Interestingly, Pope Pius XII, in the Constitution in which he solemnly defined her Assumption, carefully refrained from stating at any

39

point [5] that she died. He used instead such expressions as "at the end of her earthly course." Vatican II closely imitates the language of Pius XII, [6] wishing not to commit itself on this question.

We may be certain however that she felt within herself two conflicting drives: she would desire most intensely to see her Son, to be with Him again; she could say most ardently with St. Paul, [7] "I desire to be dissolved and to be with Christ," yet she would equally desire that His will and the will of the Father be done, and so, that her reunion should come precisely when He wanted, not when she wanted.

Should we say that she, being free from original sin, was also free of the disordered desires that are its effects? Certainly yes. But it would not be a disordered desire for her to wish to be with her Son, just as it was not a disorderly desire for Him to pray to His Father in Gethsemani: [8] "Let this chalice pass from me." His human nature, being fully human, would most naturally shrink from death and suffering. There is no disorder in such a revulsion. Yet He added: [9] "But not as I will, but as you will." Similarly she must have desired intensely to see Him, yet she added: "Not as I will, but as you will."

St. Francis de Sales [10] thinks that her desire to see Him eventually became so strong that it finally swept her soul away, causing her to die of love. St. John of the Cross, the mystics' mystic, would probably agree. For he explains how even souls of lesser perfection can literally die of love: [11] ... if others die a death caused by infirmity or length of days, in the case of these persons, even though they die in infirmity, or in old age, it is not these things that snatch away their spirits but some attack and encounter of love that is loftier than the previous ones, and more strong and powerful, for it has been able to break the web and to carry off the jewel, the soul. And so, the death of such persons is more sweet and gentle than was their spiritual life their whole life long, for they die with more lofty attacks and more delectable encounters of love, being like the swan, which sings more sweetly when it is dying."

We should add, however, with St. Francis de Sales, that even though this death from love may come in violent assaults of love in other souls, yet in Mary it was but a gentle process. For, he explains, in her, love found no resistance, and so, no need to deliver forceful attacks.

Of course, we are not certain that her death was of this sort. The mere fact that some souls of lesser perfection than was hers, died in this manner does not suffice to prove the nature of her passing. Should we say that her Son found approaching death a source of distress and heaviness, as the Gospels tell us in their description of Gethsemani and so she too may have suffered? Neither would this prove a point. For His distress was brought on not merely at the thought of death, but mostly if not entirely by the thought of sin, sin which offends His Father, which He was to take on. Further, she had already had her agony, worse than death, with Him, at the cross.

Whatever be the mode of her passing, with or without death, and in whatever kind of death, we do know that at once she was taken up body and soul into heaven. Vatican II teaches the fact of her Assumption. But it does not expand on the theme. Part of the reason would be the fact that, as the Council announced early in Chapter 8, it did not intend to treat all parts of Marian doctrine. But also, the recent document of Pius XII defining the Assumption was so brilliant that anything further might seem an anticlimax.

Before that papal Constitution appeared, there was great eagerness and speculation among theologians. There was no question that the Assumption had been a fact: the entire Church had believed that, without question, ever since the Patristic age. And, as Vatican II tells us, such an universal belief, even if held for a much shorter period, would be infallible of itself, equivalent to a solemn definition: [12] "The entire body of the faithful, being anointed by the Holy One, cannot be deceived in its belief."

But theologians were concerned to discover how this teaching could be found in the sources of revelation. If we look to the explicit teaching of Scripture, there is obviously no mention of the Assumption. Patristic documents do speak much of it. But they begin to do so rather late, and the statements of the Fathers then seem more likely to be repeating Apocryphal stories than to be serving as witnesses to a revelation coming down from the age of the Apostles.

This difficulty of finding the Assumption in the sources was so great that one noted Patrologist had the rashness to publish an article, about six months before the definition, trying to prove a definition could not be given.

It is fascinating, for this reason, to study the precise way in which Pope Pius XII managed to find the Assumption in revelation.

The Pope opened by noting the relation of the Assumption to the Immaculate Conception: [13] "For these two privileges are most closely related to each other. Christ overcame sin and death by His own death; and one who is reborn in a heavenly way through baptism has, through Christ Himself, conquered sin and death. However, in accord with His general rule, God does not wish to grant the full effect of victory over death to the just until the end of time . . . Yet God wished that the Blessed Virgin Mary be exempt from this general law. For she, by a completely singular privilege, conquered sin in her Immaculate Conception, and thus was not liable to that law of remaining in the corruption of the grave, nor did she have to wait for the end of time for the redemption of her body."

The thought is intriguing: the Pope seems, at first sight to say that since Mary was free of original sin, she must be free of a certain effect of original sin, namely, that of having to wait until the end of time for the resurrection of the body. But further reflection shows us a problem: the argument would prove more than Pius XII wants to prove. For we could reason similarly: being free of original sin, she had to be free of death too, for that is an effect of original sin. But we know he went to great lengths to avoid saying anywhere, in his own words, that she died. Hence he cannot mean it this way.

How is it possible not to mean it thus? For this reason: Liability to death, and delayed resurrection are indeed effects of original sin, but in a special way. By that sin we lost *two different kinds* of privileges: the *supernatural* gift of grace, and the *preternatural* gifts of immortality of the body and freedom from suffering and varied other evils. Now it is obvious: Exemption from original sin certainly implies deliverance from the supernatural damage of privation of the gift of grace. But it would not have to mean deliverance from the other privations. Really, her Divine Son did not, because of His freedom from original sin, spare Himself from suffering and death, which are effects of original sin. So it is not only not proved, but not even likely that she would be exempt from those trials either.

The Pope then goes on to tell of his own practice of collegiality long before Vatican II spoke of such a thing: Before making the definition, he consulted every Bishop in the world, and found them virtually unanimous in teaching this doctrine. Such a universal teaching and belief is, of course, a proof in itself that the Assumption is revealed. But it does not yet show us precisely *where* in the sources of revelation the Assumption could be found. Hence there was need of further search.

Pius XII then went on to survey the teachings of the Fathers, and of the Medieval theologians on her Assumption, and then, moving on to still later times, he found the words of St. Francis de Sales deserving special attention: [14] "St. Francis de Sales, after stating that it would be wrong to doubt that Jesus Christ kept in the most perfect way the divine command that children honour their parents, puts this question: 'What son, if he could, would not bring his mother back to life, and take her, after death, into paradise?' "

Did the Pope take this reasoning as a *conclusive proof* of the Assumption, or merely as a *fitting* reason? It seems far more likely that he considered it as the latter.

It is not likely that Pius XII intended any of these reasons just mentioned as the chief basis for his definition. But there is still one most ingenious passage to examine: [15] "We must remember especially that, since the second century, the Virgin Mary has been presented by the Holy Fathers as the New Eve, who, although subject to the New Adam, was most clearly associated with Him in that struggle against the infernal enemy which, as foretold in the proto-evangelium, was to result in that most complete victory over sin and death, which are always associated with each other in the writings of the Apostle of the Gentiles."

A rather long and heavy sentence. It is best to digest it before continuing. The Pope recalls for us the New Eve teaching of the Fathers. We begin to wonder: Will he say that since the old Eve, if she had been faithful, would not have had to wait for a delayed resurrection, then the New Eve, who was entirely faithful, should have had the favour that the old Eve would have gained? At first sight it might seem his thought was moving in that direction.

But then he begins to tell us that she, as foretold in Genesis 3:15 ("I will put enmity between you and the woman, between her Seed and your seed. He will strike your head") was closely bound with the New Adam, her Son, in the struggle against sin. That struggle was, of course, the great sacrifice of Calvary. It led to victory over sin and death. So we see that a different aspect of the New Eve theme is in the Pope's mind. It is her cooperation in the Redemption, as the New Eve with the New Adam. So he continues: "Wherefore, just as the glorious resurrection of Christ was an essential part and final sign of this victory, so also that struggle which was common to the Blessed Virgin and her Son had to be closed by the 'glorification' of her virginal body..."

The thought is both brilliant and difficult, because it is so closely knit. Pius XII tells us that Christ's death and resurrection are really *both* part of the total victory. His death brought the glorification of resurrection to Him. But, and here is the key to the argument, His great sacrificial death, which the Pope again calls the "struggle" was a work that was "*common* to the Blessed Virgin and her Son." A work in *common* should bring a result in *common*. To Him the struggle brought the glorification of the resurrection: hence to her, it strictly "*had to*" bring the glorification of the assumption.

Or, more simply: a common cause had to have a common effect. The cause was common to Jesus and Mary. It brought the common effect of glorification to both.

Here, then, is the way to find the assumption in the sources of revelation. It is found in the New Eve teaching of the Fathers. It is contained in the fact of her cooperation in redeeming us, a cooperation so close, and understood in so strict a sense, that the great sacrifice was a work that was "common" to both.

We see a double gain from this brilliant stroke of analysis: we have not only found the assumption in revelation. We also find something about the nature of her cooperation in the Redemption. Her cooperation must not be taken in just some vague loose sense. That would not allow us to conclude that her glorification *had to* follow. So her cooperation in the Redemption must be understood in a most strict sense: Else a solemn definition would lack support.

We can see that the analysis we made of her cooperation in chapter 3 was not at all excessive. Anything less would hardly satisfy the solemnly defined conclusion of the assumption constitution.

Finally, as Vatican II adds, after she was taken up, she [16] "was exalted as Queen of the universe by the Lord, so that she might be more fully conformed to her Son, the Lord of Lords, and victor over sin and death." Now, as Pius XII expressed it: [17] "Jesus is King of the eternal ages by nature and by conquest; through Him, with Him, and subordinate to Him, Mary is Queen by grace, by divine kinship, by conquest, and by singular choice. And her domain is as vast as that of her Son and God, for nothing is exempt from her dominion."

NOTES

1. Jn. 19,27.

2. On the Church § 59.

3. St. John Damascene, Oration 2,2: **Patrologia Graeca** 96,725.

4. Cf. Walter J. Burghardt, "The Testimony of the Patristic Age Concerning Mary's Death" in: **Marian Studies** 8 (1957) 58-99.

5. Pius XII never said in his own words that she died, though he did quote others who used such words.

6. On the Church § 59.

7. Phil. 1,23.

8. Mt. 26,39.

9. **Ibid.**

10. **Treatise on the Devout Life** 7,13-14.

11. **Living Flame of Love** 1,30.

12. On the Church § 12.

13. Pius XII, **Munificentissimus Deus,** Nov. 1, 1950: AAS 42, 754.

14. AAS 42, 766.

15. AAS 42, 768.

16. On the Church § 59.

17. Pius XII, **Bendito seia,** May 13, 1946: AAS 38, 266. We notice that the same expression "by right of conquest" is used to refer to both Mary and Jesus, with only due subordination of her to him expressed. So, there should be no other reservation. Hence, the implication of cooperation in the full sense.

6 — ALL-PERVADING ROLE

A picture of startling sweep develops before our eyes when we assemble the teachings of Vatican II on Mary. As we examined each individual facet of those teachings, we found more than one remarkable truth. But the total picture is something that we would scarcely have expected to find.

The Council begins its painting by speaking of the eternal divine plans, formed before the beginning of creation: [1] "The Blessed Virgin, planned for from eternity as the Mother of God along with the Incarnation of the divine Word was the loving Mother of the Redeemer on this earth, His generous associate, more than others, and the humble servant of the Lord (61) . . . she is already prophetically foreshadowed in the promise given our first parents of a victory over the serpent. Similarly, she is the Virgin who is to conceive and bear a Son, whose name is to be called Emmanuel (55)" as Isaiah the prophet foretold. [2] "The Father of Mercies willed that the acceptance of the planned-for Mother should come before the Incarnation, so that in this way, just as a woman contributed to death, [3] so also a woman should contribute to life (56)." "This union of the Mother with the Son in the work of salvation is evident from the time of the virginal conception of Christ even to His death. In the first place, it is evident when Mary, arising in haste to visit Elizabeth, is greeted as blessed by her, because of her faith in the salvation that was promised . . . [it is evident] when the Mother of God joyfully displayed her firstborn, who did not lessen but consecrated her virginal integrity, to the shepherds and the Magi. [It is evident] when she presented Him to the Lord in the temple, offering the gift of the poor, and when she heard Simeon foretelling that her Son would be a sign of contradiction, and that the sword would pierce her Mother's heart so that the thoughts of many hearts would be revealed (57) ... In the public life of Jesus, His Mother appears remarkably. [She does this] at the very beginning [of His public life] when, at the wedding in Cana of Galilee, moved by pity, she obtained by her intercession the beginning of the miracles of Jesus the Messiah. During the course of His preaching, she received His words in which He, her Son, praised the Kingdom [of God] more than the ties of flesh and blood, proclaimed blessed those who heard the Word of God and kept it, as she herself was faithfully doing ... In faith she bore with her union with her Son even to the cross, where she stood in accord with the divine plan, greatly grieved with her Only-begotten, and joined herself to His sacrifice with a Motherly heart, consenting to the immolation of the victim that had been born of her (58)." "... in suffering with her Son as He died on the Cross, she cooperated in the work of the Saviour in an altogether singular way, by obedience, faith, hope, and burning love, to restore supernatural life to souls. As a result, she is our mother in the order of grace (61)" " ... before the day of Pentecost, we see the Apostles 'persevering with one heart in prayer with the women and with Mary the Mother of Jesus and His brothers,' and Mary too with her prayers imploring the gift of the Spirit, who already at the Annunciation had overshadowed her. Finally the Immaculate Virgin ... having finished the course of her earthly life, was taken up, body and soul, to heavenly glory and was exalted as Queen of the universe by the Lord, so that she might be more fully conformed to her Son, the Lord of Lords and victor over sin and death (59)."

The key to the thought of the Council is in its insistence that the [4] "union of the Mother with the Son in the work of salvation is evident from the time of the virginal conception of Christ even to His death." Actually the Council extends this union in both directions. For it speaks of her as being "planned for from eternity" along with Him, and, of course, now that she has been "exalted as Queen of the universe ... so that she might be more fully conformed to her Son the Lord of Lords", her union with Him will never cease. It stretches out without bound into the endless expanse of eternity. In between the two "eternities", if we may use such an expression, the Council carefully goes through each of the mysteries of the life and work of her divine Son for the salvation of men. In each case it points out that her union with Him is evident.

Really, we could picture the sweep of the conciliar thought best by a great graph, a graph on which there would be two lines. One would represent the life and mysteries of the divine Redeemer, from the eternal plans, throughout time, and back again into an unceasing eternity of glory. The other line would be inferior to His, but yet parallel, closely matching, at every point. That line would represent her union with Him. As the dogmatic Constitution on the Assumption said, she is "always sharing His lot."

Or, to make it still clearer, we could pick just one word to describe the place that the Father willed to give her in the entire economy of His dealings with us: her place is *all-pervading*. There is nowhere where she is not evident, evident in union with Her Son. The Father could have done everything without her: He needed no creature. Yet He freely willed to have her cooperation at every point. Strictly speaking, He could have arranged a Redemption without Him too, as we saw in chapter 3. For He could have forgiven all sin without any reparation. Or He could have accepted a finite, an inadequate reparation. And even supposing (what is true) that the Father willed a completely adequate satisfaction, that could have been had, and had infinitely, by the incarnation in a palace, with Redemption by a brief prayer, without the death of His Son. But the Father, as we saw, literally wanted to go beyond infinity, because His plans are measured, if we may speak of measure at all, not by mathematics, but by generosity. So He freely willed to have Mary take part in the entire work of salvation, bringing her activity in at all points.

Once we see this, a remarkable conclusion emerges. Since, as is evident, we can do nothing better than to imitate the ways of the Father, then, the *ideal* response we could make to His generosity would be to imitate His ways. He has given her an all-pervading role in all His dealings with us; we could, ideally, give her a similarly all-pervading place in our response to His generosity. That would mean a spiritual life permeated with the Marian element. Really, in its full form, it would be to make, and then really live out a consecration to her.

Did the Council really favour Marian consecration? The answer is: Yes. For two reasons. First, it told us: 5 "Let the faithful remember that true devotion does not consist in sterile and passing emotion, not in a sort of empty gullibility, but that it proceeds from true faith, by which we are led to acknowledge the loftiness of the Mother of God, and are aroused to a filial love towards our Mother and to an imitation of her virtues."

We note especially the teaching that devotion must rest on and be grounded in true faith, that is, in solid doctrine. It is obvious from the picture we have assembled in this chapter from the very words of the Council that a full consecration is precisely what most logically flows from the conciliar teaching on the position God has assigned her.

But still further, the Council most explicitly said: [6] "This most Holy Synod deliberately teaches this Catholic doctrine [which it gave in the preceding parts of chapter 8 of the Constitution on the Church] and it admonishes all the sons of the Church that they should cultivate generously devotion, especially liturgical devotion, towards the Blessed Virgin, and that they should consider of great importance the practices and exercises of piety toward her that were recommended by the Magisterium over the course of centuries..." But, the Magisterium often had recommended consecration to her. In fact, on the very day on which this brilliant chapter 8 on Mary was promulgated at the Council, Pope Paul VI arose in the Council itself and said: [7] "... our eyes turn to the whole world ... which our Predecessor Pius XII ... not without heavenly inspiration, solemnly consecrated to the Immaculate Heart of the Virgin Mary ... We too entrust the whole human race, along with its difficulties and anxieties ... to the care of the heavenly Mother, to be protected. O Virgin Mary, Mother of God, Most August Mother of the Church, to You we commend the entire Church and the Ecumenical Council."

On May 13, 1967, on the occasion of his unprecedented personal pilgrimage to the great Marian sanctuary of Fatima, Paul VI issued an Apostolic Exhortation in which he recalled again how Pius XII, 25 years before, consecrated the world to the Immaculate Heart [8] "[a consecration] which we ourselves repeated on November 21, 1964 [at the Council]." And he added: "... we urge all the sons of the Church that they individually consecrate themselves again to the Immaculate Heart of the Mother of the Church, and, by extending this outstanding sign of devotion into their lives, become more and more conformed to the divine will, and, devoutly imitating the examples of their heavenly Queen, they serve her as sons."

Of course, there are many degrees in the practice of Marian consecration. It is one thing to point out how brilliantly *logical* and *ideal* it is to live out a full consecration, as a means of imitating the ways of the Father Himself, who gave and gives her an all-pervading role. It is another thing to say that *all* are obliged to carry it out in the fullest way. Objectively, to do so is the best — the doctrinal picture given by Vatican II, on which it says real devotion should be grounded, makes that clear. But yet not all are given the same *kind* of graces, not all are equally adapted.

At least, it is clear from the Council that all should do something, even rather much. To try to ignore her, to call for the decline of interest in her and devotion to her would be not only to go contrary to Vatican II, it would be to fly in the face of the divine plans themselves.

NOTES

1. The following passage consists of quotations from Chapter 8 of On the Church.

2. Is. 7,14.

3. This is the New Eve theme we saw in Chapter 1 above.

4. On the Church § 57.

5. **Ibid.** § 67.

6. **Ibid.** § 67.

7. Address of Nov. 21, 1964, as found in AAS 56,1017.

8. Paul VI, **Signum magnum,** May 13, 1967: AAS 59,475.

7 — MODEL OF THE CHURCH

To live out the implications of the ideal that flows with such logic from the doctrinal picture painted by Vatican II, we would begin by imitating the qualities of Mary. With this in mind, Vatican II presents her as the "Type of the Church." That word "Type" is used in two closely related senses: She is the prophecy-in-action of what the Church was to become, and still has not fully attained; she is the model for the Church, for the Church as a whole, and for each member of the Church.

To understand what a *type* means, we need to go back to the Old Testament and to the interpretations of it given by the early Fathers of the Church. The Fathers saw two kinds of prophecies in the Old Testament: prophecies made *in words*, and prophecies made by *actions*, or by the very *existence* of persons or things.

We need not delay on prophecies in words: everyone is familiar with that category. But the prophecies made by actions, which are *types*, need a bit of explanation. The situation is most easily seen through a few examples. Isaac, carrying the wood on which he himself was to be sacrificed, is a type of Christ carrying His cross. The ark, holding all who were saved from the deluge, is a type of the Church, which is the means of salvation from the waters of eternal destruction.

Somewhat similarly, the Council can speak of Mary as a Type of the Church: [1] "The Mother of God is a Type of the Church, as St. Ambrose already taught, that is, [she is a Type] in the order of faith, love, and perfect union with Christ."

Mary is a Type who foretold what the Church was to be in two chief respects: she is both virgin and Mother. So too is the Church: [2] "By believing and obeying, she begot the very Son of the Father on earth. She did not know man, but was overshadowed by the Holy Spirit, and, as the New Eve, she put her doubt-free faith in the messenger of God, not in the ancient serpent. She brought forth a Son whom God made the first-born [3] among many brothers, that is, the faithful, in whose birth and development she cooperates with a motherly love."

The Council continues, showing how the Church follows after the Type or pattern of Mary in both respects. Mary was the Virgin who became a Mother by her faith; so too the Church: [4] "Now the Church, contemplating her hidden holiness and imitating her love, and faithfully carrying out the will of the Father, likewise becomes a Mother by faithfully receiving the Word of God."

We note the fruitful play on the expression "receiving the Word of God." Mary received the Word of God in two senses: she received the words of the angel and obeyed them; she thereby conceived the Divine Word, that is, the second Person of the Most Blessed Trinity.

Similarly the Church: [5] "by her preaching and by baptism, she [the Church] brings forth to new life Sons, conceived of the Holy Spirit, and born of God. And she too is a virgin, who keeps wholly and purely the fidelity she has pledged to her Spouse [the Holy Spirit], and, in imitating the Mother of her Lord, by the power of the Holy Spirit, in a virginal fashion keeps integral faith, solid hope, sincere love [for Him]."

However, in the case of Old Testament types, that

which came first was less perfect than the later fulfillment. But when the Council calls Mary the Type of the Church, it openly proclaims that the Church falls short of its type: [6] "In the Blessed Virgin, the Church has already reached that perfection in which she is [7] 'without spot or wrinkle'. But the faithful are still struggling to grow in holiness by overcoming sin. And so they lift up their eyes to Mary, who shines forth to the whole community of the elect as the model of virtues."

In speaking of the perfect holiness of the Church, we need to distinguish two senses in which we could use the word *Church*. If we think of the Church in an almost abstract way, as the means established by Christ to bring men to holiness, a means that in itself possesses all power of sanctification, in that sense we can see the Church is already fully holy. But we can also, and more often do, think of the Church more concretely, as the totality of the Members of Christ the Head. The Council in the statement we have just read is thinking of the Church in this second way. Speaking within this category, we must, of course, recognize that no member or group of members of the Church ever has or ever will reach the perfection of holiness and love that Mary has already attained. We think spontaneously of the brilliant words of Pius IX. Because the Eternal Father planned to make her the Mother of His only Son, says the Pope, [8] "He marvelously heaped upon her, more than on all angelic spirits and all the Saints, an abundance of all heavenly favours taken from the treasury of the divinity, so that she, always absolutely free from every stain of sin, and entirely beautiful and perfect, showed forth such a fulness of innocence and holiness that none greater under God can be thought of, and no one but God can comprehend it."

In no possible sense could the Church hope to attain

so dazzling a height that only God Himself can know fully what it is!

No wonder then that the Council adds: [9] "The Church, devoutly thinking on her, and contemplating her in the light of the Word-made-man, reverently enters more deeply into the supreme mystery of the incarnation, and is made more and more conformed to her Spouse... The Church, following after the glory of Christ, is made more like to her exalted Type, constantly advancing in faith, hope and love, and seeking and carrying out the divine will in all things."

We might have thought the Council would be content with its long and beautiful presentation of Mary as the model of the Church. But no, what it said in a general way for the whole Church, it wanted to restate individually for each of the chief groups within the Church.

To those engaged in the lay apostolate, the Council says: [10] "The perfect model of this spiritual and apostolic life is the Most Blessed Virgin Mary, the Queen of Apostles, who, while she lived on earth the life common to all, filled with labours and care of her family, was always most closely joined with her Son, and cooperated in the work of the Saviour in an entirely singular way. Moreover now, assumed into heaven [11] 'by her motherly love she takes care of the brothers of her Son who are still on the way [to their eternal home] and who are involved in dangers and difficulties, until they are led to the blessed Fatherland.' Let all most devoutly honour her, and commend their life and apostolate to her motherly care."

Missionaries are urged to look upon her as the Queen of Apostles: [12] "Realizing that it is God who brings it about that His Kingdom comes on earth, let them [missionaries] pour forth their prayers together with all the faithful, that through the intercession of the Virgin Mary, Queen of

Apostles, the nations may be led as soon as possible to the knowledge of the truth . . ."

As if in special insistence, the Council twice, in two different documents, urges religious to follow Mary: [13] ". . . the [evangelical] counsels . . . contribute more than a little to spiritual freedom, they continually arouse the fervour of love, and especially, they are able to make the Christian person more and more conformed to the virginal way of life in poverty which Christ the Lord chose for Himself, and which His Virgin Mother embraced . . ." [14] "And so, by the prayers of the most sweet Virgin Mary Mother of God [15] 'whose life is the instruction of all,' may they daily make progress, and bring further richer salutary fruits."

Seminarians are on the way to becoming Priests, who are called "other Christs". Precisely because he is another Christ, the Priest is in a more special way a son of the Mother of Christ. To Seminarians the Council says: [16] "Let them honour and love with the confidence of sons, the Most Blessed Virgin Mary, who was given as a Mother to the disciple by Christ Jesus as He died on the cross."

To Priests themselves the Council repeats the same advice: [17] "They will always find a marvelous model of such docility [to the Holy Spirit] in the Blessed Virgin Mary who, led by the Holy Spirit, devoted herself totally to the mystery of the Redemption of men. Let priests love and honour with the devotion of sons, this Mother of the Eternal High Priest, the Queen of Apostles, and the protector of their ministry."

Finally, in the document renewing the liturgy, the Council added: [18] "In celebrating this annual cycle of the Mysteries of Christ, Holy Church venerates the Blessed Mary, the Mother of God, with special love, she who is bound in an indissoluble bond with her Son in the work of Salvation. In her she admires and praises the most splendid fruit of the Redemption, and, as in a most pure image, contemplates that which she herself desires and joyfully hopes to be." "Meanwhile", as the Council said in its Constitution on the Church, [19] "just as the Mother of Jesus, already glorified in body and soul in heaven, is the image, and the beginning of the Church-to-be-perfected in the world to come, so on earth, until the day of the Lord comes, she [Mary] shines forth as a sure sign of hope and consolation to the People of God still on the way [to the heavenly fatherland]."

NOTES

1. On the Church § 63.

2. **Ibid.** § 63.

3. Rom. 8,29.

4. On the Church § 64.

5. **Ibid.** § 64.

6. **Ibid.** § 65.

7. Eph. 5,27.

8. Pius IX, **Ineffabilis Deus,** Dec. 8, 1854.

9. On the Church § 65.

10. On the lay apostolate § 4

11. Quoting On the Church § 62.

12. On missions § 42.

13. On the Church § 46.

14. On the Religious Life § 25.

15. St. Ambrose, **De Virginitate** 2,2,15.

16. On Seminarians § 8.

17. On Priests § 18.

18. On Liturgy § 103.

19. On the Church § 68.

8 — VIRGIN MOST FAITHFUL

A problem arises when we begin to take the advice of the Council to heart, and seriously begin to study the details of imitating the virtues of Mary. For we recall how often in the passages we have quoted so far, the Council places great stress on her faith and obedience: it speaks more often of these than it does of her love. Now of course no one denies that love is the greatest of all virtues. So we must ask why the Council chose to stress her faith so greatly.

We can make a beginning by noticing how the Council describes faith itself. The word had long been used in a rather narrow sense of intellectual acceptance of a truth given us by God. The Council of course does not mean to object to that use of the word *faith:* usage has surely sanctioned it. But the Council prefers to go back to an older way of speaking, one which it forms by putting together the many things St. Paul says about faith, to form a synthesis, a unified picture. In the Constitution on Divine Revelation we find this: [1] "We must give to God the [2] 'obedience of faith' in which a man freely commits himself wholly to God." So faith is really the total adherence of a man to God. What would that entail? Chiefly three things, depending on the situation. If God speaks a truth, we adhere totally to Him by *intellectual acceptance* of that truth. This is, of course, the sense in which faith has been employed so much in modern times. But there is more: if God makes a promise total adherence means absolute *confidence* that He will keep that promise. If He gives us a command, then we adhere by *obedience* to that command. Of course, all these things—intellectual belief, confidence, obedience—are to be carried out in love.

St. Paul, from whom the Council takes this fuller conception of faith, speaks often of the faith of Abraham. When he was ninety-nine years old, and his wife Sara was of similar age, and sterile at that, Abraham was given a vision in which God promised to make him the Father of a great nation through a son yet to be born, Isaac. Humanly, such a thing seemed impossible. Yet Abraham did not hesitate, he put full faith in God. His faith entailed both intellectual belief of God's word, and confidence in His promise. Because of this faith, says St. Paul, Abraham was just in the sight of God. A few years later, a further trial of faith came to Abraham. That son Isaac had been born, but was still only a young boy. Abraham had believed the word of God saying that he was to be the father of a great nation through Isaac. But then God appeared again, told Abraham to take that son Isaac and offer him in sacrifice on a nearby mountain. Before, Abraham had been asked only for intellectual acceptance and confidence. Now there is added a demand for obedience, an obedience that was most difficult. He was to sacrifice his son. But the difficulty was not only that coming from the natural love of a father for his son: there was the impossibility, humanly it would seem that way, of reconciling God's promise of a great posterity through Isaac with the command to kill Isaac as a sacrifice before the promise could even begin to be fulfilled.

A lesser soul probably would have felt fully justified in saying to God: "Now I want to do your will. You have told me to believe I will be the father of a nation through Isaac. You have commanded me to kill Isaac as a sacrifice.

Obviously, I cannot do both. So I beg you to tell me which one you wish me to do. I am ready to do either one."

But Abraham did not question, did not seek to see how the two incompatible demands could be reconciled. He simply went ahead and began to do what God had commanded. He knew both things had to be done: it was enough to know God willed both. It was not necessary to understand, to see the *how*.

This was a faith that had to work in the dark, that is, to go ahead without being able to see, to adhere to God when it seemed impossible to carry out His will. When there are little or no obstacles present, not much force is required to adhere to God: faith does not have to be strong. But Abraham was placed in a situation in which he had to either have a faith of heroic strength, or to fail utterly in faith.

To judge from this and many other incidents in Scripture, [3] God often is pleased to put human beings to such a test. It is not that He wants them to suffer: rather, it is because in His love He wants them to grow spiritually. Then He will be able to give much more lavishly of His love and favours to them.

If we think only superficially of the relation of Mary to her Divine Son, we might think all would be sweetness and light, all would be easy and full of every delight. But, precisely because He loved her more than all angels and saints, He wanted to enrich her to the maximum. As a result, He placed her many times in situations that demanded a great faith, a faith that would adhere to God even in the darkness of impossibility.

It all began with the annunciation. We call it a joyful mystery, and so it is. But we must not forget that the joys of this life are often mixed with difficulties, even sorrows. The annunciation was a blend of joy with extreme difficulty.

She, like all devout Jews, had been taught, with insistent emphasis, that there is only one God. Now the angel told her that the Holy Spirit would "overshadow" her. To one who had long meditated on Scripture, that word would easily recall how the divine presence had overshadowed and filled the tabernacle in the desert. The angel added: *"For this reason,* the holy one to be born will be called Son of God." The connection St. Luke records is important: Precisely because she was to be overshadowed and filled with the divine Spirit, for that reason, her Child would be the Son of God.

Here a seemingly impossible demand appeared before her eyes: on the one hand, she knew, she had to believe there is only *one* God; on the other hand, the archangel told her her Son would be God.

Some modern commentators have reasoned this way: She could not possibly have accepted both points. We can, for we know the distinctions of later theology, especially those given us by the Council of Chalcedon (451 A.D.) about the two natures and one person in Christ and about the one nature and three persons in God. But, they say, Mary did not know these distinctions. Therefore, she could not have accepted. Therefore, she could not have understood that her Son was to be divine.

What these commentators forget is how faith works. Faith is at its strongest when it must hold on in the dark, in the face of seeming impossibility. Abraham did not say: "I can either believe I will have a great posterity through Isaac; or I can sacrifice him. But I cannot do both." Abraham simply went ahead, holding to both, without knowing how it could be done. Similarly Mary, far stronger in faith, could hold to both truths, the unity of God, and the divinity of her Son-to-be, even though she could not understand. For that matter, neither do we understand the Blessed Trinity, even after so many centuries of Councils and of theologizing.

Further reason for thinking she did know His divinity appears when we notice that not long after the annunciation, Elizabeth [4] "filled with the Holy Spirit" as St. Luke says exclaimed: [5] "How does it happen to me that the Mother of my Lord comes to me?" That word *Lord* at that time commonly meant God. The ancient Greek version of the Old Testament regularly used the word *Kyrios, Lord,* to translate the most sacred name, *Yahweh.* Now, is it likely that Elizabeth should know, and Mary should not? Again, since Mary meditated so much on the Old Testament, would she not have understood the words of Isaiah [6] who said that the Messiah was to be *El gibbor,* that is, *God the Mighty?* Of course, many say that the Jews in general at that time did not understand. Probably they are right (though there is the puzzling, and eloquent, silence of the Greek version [7] of the Old Testament, which simply refuses to translate *El gibbor* at all) apparently, finding it impossible to reconcile with the unity of God. What the weak faith of the translators could not comprehend, Mary's strong faith would surely take in.

We should add this: our Scripture scholars have long insisted, and rightly, that we should interpret the meaning of a Scriptural expression in light of the use of the same expression throughout all Scripture. Now that phrase, *El gibbor* does occur elsewhere in the Old Testament. *Every time* it occurs, it means always and only one thing: *God the Mighty.* So why not in Isaiah?

And we should also notice that the same commentators today tend much to deny that Christ Himself knew who He was, until rather late in His life. They say He Himself did not know He was divine. This is really not a new advance in theology: it is an ancient error, condemned long ago, in 553 A.D. by Pope Vigilius, [8] in the aftermath of Nestorianism, which said there were two persons in Christ. If there were two persons in Him, it would follow that the human person might not know he was joined to a divine Person. It would make Christ practically schizoid, a split personality: two persons inhabiting one body.

Now history shows that Mary and her Divine Son are joined in theology as well as in the work of Redemption. Errors about Him normally imply errors about her. And so it seems to be in regard to her knowledge. If He did not know who He was, naturally, neither should she.

Whatever one may think about her knowledge at the annunciation, we cannot doubt the trials of faith she had to undergo so many times. To have to rescue a child, who was at least the powerful Messiah, by fleeing into Egypt; to have the most obedient of sons suddenly seem to turn, and cause what would appear needless anguish in the three days loss before He was found in the Temple; to have that same Son seem to reject a very charitable request of hers at Cana: [9] "What is it to you and to me?"; to have Him seem to reject her, when she came to the edge of the crowd to see Him, when He said: [10] "Who is my Mother?" Of course, we know she must have understood, when He added: [11] "Whoever does the will of my Father in heaven, is my brother and sister and mother." As Vatican II said, referring to this very incident: [12] "she received His words in which He, her Son, praised the Kingdom [of God] more than the ties of flesh and blood, and proclaimed blessed those who heard the word of God and kept it, as she herself was faithfully doing." Yet, even knowing that He was merely stressing that adherence to God in faith is more important than the dignity one holds, even if it be the dignity of the Mother of God, it still would be far from easy to accept.

But the heaviest trial of her faith came at the Cross. There, when all the Apostles except only John had given up their faith and fled, she stood firm and [13] "cooperated in the work of the Saviour ... by obedience, faith, hope, and burning love." She had to believe this besmirched, disgraced, dying wretch was really the salvation of the world. She had to [14] "consent to the immolation of the victim that had been born of her."

It would be a frightful demand to place on any Mother, to ask her to consent to the death of her Son in the obedience of faith. But that difficulty is multiplied by two factors, by the depth of the suffering she sees him undergoing, and by the love she has for Him. As for His sufferings, who can adequately describe them, whether we think of their physical aspect of fiendish torment, or the even more bitter psychological aspect of total heartless rejection? The difficulty that reached such an immense peak from seeing the intensity and depth of His suffering would be multiplied by her love for Him. How great was that? It was the love of the best of Mothers for not just the best of Sons but for a Divine Son. It was a love that, [15] as Pius IX said was so great, even at the beginning of her existence that [16] "none greater under God can be thought of, and no one but God can comprehend it."

Here then was a faith that adhered totally to God, believing His word, confident in His promise, obeying His will, in spite of a degree of difficulty which, when we carefully calculate it, is so great that only God can comprehend it — for one of the factors that multiplies that difficulty is measureless, while the other, as we have just seen, is so great that no creature can understand it: that is reserved to God Himself.

1. On Divine Revelation § 5.

2. Rom. 16,26.

3. Cf. Lk. 9,57-62; Jn. 2,4; Mk. 3,31-35; Jn. 6,51-67.

4. Lk. 1,41.

5. Lk. 1,43.

6. Is. 9,6.

7. We refer to the Septuagint, a Greek translation made about the middle of the 3rd century B.C. by Jewish scholars.

8. Cf. Denzinger-Schönmetzer, **Enchiridion Symbolorum** § 419. Cf. also the teaching of Pius XII in **Mystici Corporis,** that Christ knew and loved each of us from the first moment of the Incarnation: DS 3812 (DB 2289).

9. There are problems of translation here. Literally, the Greek would read as we have rendered it.

10. Mt. 12,48.

11. Mt. 12,50.

12. On the Church § 58.

13. On the Church § 63.

14. **Ibid.** § 58.

15. Though formally different, in practice, holiness and love of God are interchangeable terms.

16. Pius IX, **Ineffabilis Deus,** Dec. 8, 1854.

9 — LIVING BY FAITH

There are many facets to the ways in which we should try to imitate Mary's faith. Two stand out among them. First, we need to believe and to obey the Church, out of confidence in the promises the Father made through Christ. Second, we should act on faith, by taking the right attitude to creatures. We can consider one in this chapter, another in the next.

Mary believed the word of the angel: he spoke to her with the authority of God Himself. We imitate this aspect of her faith by similarly believing the word of God. But it is important to note the ways in which that word reaches us, for confusion in our time on this point is very great.

At the very start of the Protestant movement, one of the most critical and basic points of departure was concerned with this question: How do we know for certain what is the meaning of the sources of revelation? The answer given to that question really determined whether a man was a Protestant or a Catholic.

Both sides agreed on this: A person ought to diligently and prayerfully study the sources of revelation. Of course, by "sources of revelation", a Catholic would have considered both Scripture and Tradition; while a Protestant would have considered only Scripture as the source. But once that had been done, and the moment arrived for the critical decision on what really has been revealed, then came the radical split between Protestant and Catholic. For the Protestant said that the criterion, the decisive thing was simply this: What do *I* think? In other words, personal, private judgment was the final means. There was no higher court which had any right to speak after that. For the Catholic, the decisive criterion was: What does the Church teach?

Today, Protestants still hold most firmly to their original position of private judgment. But many Catholics, strange to say, no longer hold to the Catholic position: they have crossed over to the Protestant side, while still claiming to be Catholic. They commonly say that Vatican II has authorized them to follow their own judgment instead of the teaching of the Church.

In our opening chapter we saw how totally the reverse of the truth was the common notion that Vatican II had voted to downgrade Mary. On our present matter, the very common belief is equally the opposite of the truth. What the Council really taught is summed up most concisely in the Constitution on Divine revelation: [1] "The function of authoritatively interpreting the word of God, written or handed on, has been entrusted *solely* to the living Magisterium of the Church, whose authority is exercised in the name of Jesus Christ." So, if one follows Vatican II, he will not be authorized to contradict the Church and follow instead his own personal opinions. For he knows that when the final decisive moment comes to determine the meaning of revelation, to say what is true in theology, it is *solely* the teaching authority of the Church that is to decide.

Vatican II distinguishes two levels of teaching in the Church, infallible, or defined teachings, and non-infallible, non-defined teachings.

Infallible teachings can come not only from a General Council: Vatican II repeats the teaching of Vatican I that they can be given even by the Pope himself acting alone. In fact, Vatican II explicitly teaches—in spite of popular distortions to the contrary—that the Pope need not, unless he wishes, consult anyone at all, not even the Bishops, before defining: [2] "His definitions of themselves, and not from the consent of the Church, are rightly called unchangeable, for they are pronounced under the assistance of the Holy Spirit, promised him in Blessed Peter. And so they need no approval of others, nor is there room for an appeal to any other judgment."

But the Council goes much farther: it even requires that we interiorly accept and believe even non-infallible teachings of the Pope, even when he is speaking alone: [3] "... religious submission of will and of mind must be shown in a singular way to the authentic Magisterium of the Roman Pontiff even when he is not speaking ex cathedra [not defining]; that is, in such a way that... there is sincere adherence to the judgments pronounced by him, according to his manifested mind and will..."

Here is the point at which many fail, and turn to a Protestant, not a Catholic method. They say there is a legitimate right of dissent, for specialists in theology. And if one is not a specialist, he will say he is following one. Really, if a man makes that his principle of action, then even when he does actually go along with a papal teaching, his basic reason for doing so will not be the fact that it is taught by a providentially guided authority, but that it agrees with his own reasoning. In other words, the decisive thing will not be the authority of teaching, but mere human reason. To act that way is to be, logically, a Protestant. If a man were to *reason* his way to every conclusion taught by the Church, but his reason for adherence to these truths would be his own reason, not the teaching authority of the Church, such a man, even though he believed everything the Church teaches, would be logically a Protestant.

Many say: "I cannot see it. So how can I accept it?

70

I must follow my conscience." This is not the way of Mary, nor is it the way of any real Catholic. She accepted the word of God's messenger, not because she reasoned herself to the same conclusion, but simply because that messenger spoke with the authority of God. Similarly, the reason why we should accept the teaching of the Church should be the divinely protected teaching authority. We accept, not because of our reasonings, however good (it is, of course, good to *add* the support of reason), but because of *faith* in the promises of Christ who said: [4] "He who hears you, hears me, and he who sets you aside, sets me aside." And: "If he will not hear the Church, let him be to you as a pagan and a publican."

So our support in accepting these teachings is, ultimately, faith, not reason. That fact removes a great difficulty. For many persons have a low esteem for the personal intelligence, holinesss, capability of the Pope and the collective Bishops. But if one has faith in the words of Christ, he cares not at all whether this particular Pope is intelligent, holy, highly competent. All that is strictly irrelevant. The *only thing that is decisive* is that he is the recipient today of the promises of Christ: "He who hears you, hears me."

Nor should one plead "After all, it is admitted that these teachings are not infallible. So there is room for doubt." Yes, there is an outside chance. There is also such a chance that the food we will eat this evening that comes from a can is infected with Botulism: but normal persons do not worry about that, for the possibility is so very remote. Far more remote is the chance that a non-infallible teaching could err. And if it should, what would place us in the better position when we must make our accounting before Christ the Judge? Would it be better to say: "My policy was to follow those whom you promised to protect", or: "I was afraid that they might conceivably slip in spite of you, so I often doubted."

The second man, making a policy of following himself, will, statistically speaking, have to be wrong with some frequency; the first man might make one mistake [5] in two thousand years. Which will the Judge more readily excuse? Which is imitating the model of the faith of Mary, which the Council sets before us? [6]

But we need to look also at another aspect of faith. Following St. Paul, as we have seen, the Council includes three elements in faith: intellectual acceptance of divinely taught truth, confidence in God's promises, and obedience to His will. What we have just considered takes in the first two of these three facets of faith. Full imitation of Mary's faith and full carrying out of the Council teaching requires that we also add the third facet: obeying the Church.

Even though there is a college of Bishops, with whom the Pope may work when he so chooses, yet [7] "his power remains complete, over all, whether Pastors [Bishops] or the faithful. For the Roman Pontiff, by virtue of his position as Vicar of Christ and Shepherd of the whole Church, has full, supreme, and universal power, which he can always exercise freely." Within their own dioceses, [8] "Bishops have the sacred right and duty before the Lord, of passing laws for their subjects, or rendering judgment, and of regulating all that pertains to worship and the apostolate. ... All the faithful should embrace with prompt obedience what the sacred Pastors order ... imitating the example of Christ, who by his obedience even to death, opened the blessed way of freedom of the sons of God to all men." These last words remind us of the striking statement of the Council given earlier in the same document: [9] "By His obedience He brought about redemption."

This obedience, as we said, is one of the three aspects or parts of faith. And it is founded on the other parts of faith, that is, on our belief that Christ has given to the authorities of the Church the right to command in His name.

Here too, as in matters of belief, some persons are inclined to say: "But I cannot see it, this doesn't seem to me to be a good decision". What should we say? We need to notice that there are two facets here. First the question of whether Christ wills that we obey. There is no doubt that He does, unless of course, a command were immoral. But second: Are we obliged, if we follow the obedience of faith, to not only obey, but even to think that every command is the most prudent, the best way, or even that it is a very good way? By no means. The protection promised by Christ to the Church does not include a guarantee of prudence in all things. So it is enough for us to obey: we are not obliged to think every command very good and suitable.

But if we are honest with ourselves, we will, however, make an honest effort to see things the superior's way. For normal human pride tends to make us think a command is bad simply because we do not like to be given commands. Our feeling tends to warp our judgment. So, we are simply making a well-calculated allowance for probable error due to this tendency of ours when we honestly try to see things the superior's way. We recall too that there is offered to superiors, a grace of state. They can, and sometimes do misuse or refuse such graces. But at least the graces are offered. We are being realistic if we take that fact into account too.

Finally, we might note the example of Mary's Son. He knew the terrible hypocrisy of the Pharisees and strongly rebuked them for it. Yet He also said: [10] "The Scribes and Pharisees have taken their seat upon the seat of Moses. Therefore, all things they say to you, do and observe. But do not do as they do. For they speak and do not do. They bind heavy burdens, hard to bear, and impose them on the shoulders of men, but they themselves do not wish to move them with their finger."

Those who think ill of today's ecclesiastical authorities might ask: Are they worse than the Scribes and Pharisees, the "whitewashed sepulchres" who bind heavy loads, impose them on others, but do not touch them themselves? Even so, the divine Teacher says: "All things they say to you, do and observe." Christ Himself obeyed, even to death, even to the death of the cross. And, [11] "By His obedience, He brought about Redemption." His Mother amid the darkness of Calvary continued her obedience that called for acceptance of the death of her Son. Only strong faith, faith that grows more powerful in darkness, can do such things. Those who want to follow after Mary and Her Son will obey. Their faith will grow from strength to strength in doing so.

NOTES

1. On Divine Revelation § 10.

2. On the Church § 25.

3. **Ibid.** § 25.

4. Lk. 10,16 and Mt. 18,17.

5. Many charges are made that the Church has erred on the non-infallible level. The only charge that begins to hold is that in the Galileo case, one in 2000 years.

6. It is often said that the old traditional theology manuals used to admit a right of dissent, for a specialist, on non-defined teachings. That is true, but only if he has found new evidence, not previously known (such is not the case on Birth Control, etc.) and further and especially, he may not **persist** in that denial. He must accept the decision of the Church on his new evidence. Canon 2317 directs that if he does persist in denial, he is to be removed from preaching, hearing confessions, and from any teaching position.

7. On the Church § 22.

8. **Ibid.** § 27 and § 37.

9. **Ibid.** § 9.

10. Mt. 23,2-4.

11. On the Church § 3.

10 — LIVING OUT FAITH

In urging religious to imitate Mary, Vatican II said that the practice of the evangelical counsels of poverty, chastity, and obedience [1] "contribute more than a little to spiritual freedom. They continually arouse the fervor of love, and especially, they are able to make the Christian person more and more conformed to the virginal way of life in poverty which Christ the Lord chose for Himself, and which His Virgin Mother embraced . . ."

In following out such spiritual ideals, in varied ways and degrees according to our various states in life, we are actually acting on faith. We saw in the introduction to the last chapter that imitation of Mary's faith includes chiefly two things: first, believing and obeying the Church, out of confidence in the promises the Father gave us through His Son, and then, acting on faith. We turn now to this second way.

So the Council wants religious to imitate closely the life of poverty, virginity-celibacy, and obedience which Christ *chose* for Himself, for He alone of all men could choose all the circumstances of his daily life, which for others, even Mary, are things to be *"embraced"* from the hand of God. The Council recommends these practices because they continually arouse love, and make one more like Christ and His Mother.

Those who are not called by God to literally and most fully live a life of poverty, chastity and obedience, still can, and should, follow these counsels literally in some degree, and totally in their spirit. The reason is obvious. The whole of Christian life [2] could be summed up by saying this: A man is saved and is made holy if, and to the extent that, he is a member of Christ and is conformed to Him. No one can be saved at all, can be His disciple, unless he to some degree is like Christ. The more like Christ a man is in this life, the more he will later be like the glorious Christ.

But we want to note a special aspect of the practice of the counsels. To follow them really is a matter of faith, of living out the implications of faith. How and why that is true needs a bit of exploration.

One way to make the situation clear to ourselves is to investigate what is called the "New Spirituality." Many first became aware of such a movement with the publication of a book by J. D. Gerken, *Towards a Theology of the Layman.* Gerken asserted that if one compares two things, celibacy for a religious motive, and marriage, he should make two comments: neither one is any better in itself than the other; neither helps more for spiritual growth. To make his point, Gerken had to try to explain away so many statements in Scripture and in the documents of the Church which teach the opposite.

But actually, this view of Gerken's is just one facet of a much larger attempt at a revolution in the whole of the spiritual life. It could be summed up this way. If one compares, again, two things: to give up any creature or pleasure for a religious motive, or not to give it up, he must again make the same two comments, namely, neither one is any better in itself than the other; neither one helps more for spiritual growth.

We find indications of this basic view of the New Spirituality in many recent writings. For example, Father E. Larkin, in an article [3] on "Desacralization and Asceticism" happily wrote that in the old spirituality, one became holy by avoiding the world. But, he said, a different attitude reigns now, for the world also is "transparent of God". He meant that all creation is a manifestation of Christ, a vehicle of grace, and a means of contact with God. For, he said, the things of God are everything. Even more impressive at first sight is a footnote [4] in the Abbott edition of Vatican II that asserts that the age-old detachment of the Church from the world is no longer valid.

We must remark at once that that footnote is not by the Council, but by the editor of that translation.

But if we look at the passage of the Council [5] to which the note is attached, we will see the chief base on which the defenders of the New Spirituality attempt to rest their case. In it, the Council teaches that all creatures are good, for a triple reason. First, God made them all good, as He Himself proclaimed in the opening chapters of Genesis after creating each new thing. Second, creatures acquire an added dignity since they are for the use of man, the highest being in visible creation. Third, creatures are still further ennobled by the fact that in the Incarnation, Christ took on a created nature and used created things.

With this triple goodness of creatures as a foundation, the New Spirituality concludes: Therefore, there is no spiritual gain in giving up such good things.

We notice at once that they have made a very large leap. It is one thing to say that creatures are good; another to conclude that therefore there is no gain in foregoing any of them.

Did Vatican II really mean to teach this New Spirituality? There is no need to merely guess at the thought of the Council by making a long leap. The Council did, most directly and explicitly, say what it meant on this point. It did this chiefly by its teachings on the three evangelical counsels, for they are, actually, nothing other than the three chief ways of giving up creatures. By pov   , one gives up possessions; by chastity, he foregoes the lawful use of sex; by obedience, he relinquishes to a considerable degree, his personal freedom. At the opening of this chapter we read one statement of the Council in which the practice of these counsels is explicitly praised as a means of being like Christ, as a means of stirring up love and promoting Christian freedom. There are many other statements by the Council to the same effect.

For example, in the Constitution on the Church we read: [6] "The Church repeatedly thinks over the admonition of the Apostle, who, urging the faithful to love, exhorts them to take the attitude that was found in Christ Jesus, who 'emptied Himself, taking on the form of a slave... [and] became obedient even to death' and for us 'became poor, though he was rich.'" Similarly, in the Decree on the Missions: [7] "The Church, at the urging of the Spirit of Christ, must advance by the same way that Christ did, that is, by the way of poverty, obedience, service, and self-immolation even to death..."

So the Council actually teaches the opposite of what the New Spirituality claims it teaches! (We recall how the press reported the Council downgraded Mary, when in reality, it went farther in its Marian teaching than any Council in the entire history of the Church).

The advocates of the New Spirituality are apt to reply: "But we do approve of mortification. We merely say that there is so much of it in our lives anyway, sent us by Providence, that there is no point in imposing more mortification on ourselves by giving things up without need."

Pope Paul VI, in his decree *Poenitemini* of February 17, 1966 answers this claim: "... the Church ... invites all Christians without distinction to respond to the divine precept of penitence by some voluntary act, *in addition to the renunciation imposed by the burdens of everyday life.*" In saying this,

Pope Paul is merely following the pattern set by St. Paul, who, in writing a second time to the Corinthians, enumerated the many hardships he encountered in his work of preaching the Gospel. Yet St. Paul added [8] "fastings also".

The entire teaching of the Council and the Popes on this subject is really just a restatement of Scripture. Christ Himself in the parable of the sower pictured the good seed as falling on various types of soil. Some of it fell among thorns. It began to sprout, but then the thorns choked it. And He explained: [9] "As to that which fell among the thorns, these are the ones who hear [the word] and as they go, are choked by the cares and riches and pleasures of life, and they do not bear fruit." Now the riches and pleasures of this life are good, even triply good. But they can at the same time be thorns, that is, they can be a danger to spiritual development. That is why He also promised: [10] "And everyone who has left houses or brothers or sisters, or father, or mother, or wife, or children, or lands for the sake of my name, will receive a hundredfold and will inherit everlasting life."

We can see now how the Council can say that all creatures are good, triply good, but that still, there is a spiritual gain in giving them up: even good things can have disadvantages or can bring dangers. Or, to look at another aspect of the same reality, there are two scales on which we can rate creatures, the absolute scale, and the relative scale. On the absolute scale, rating creatures *in themselves,* we must say that they are all good. But on the relative scale, that is *comparing their goodness with the things to come* in the future life, we must say they are very slight indeed, and that if they cause a danger, it is better to have rather little to do with them.

St. Paul understood this relative scale well. He told the Romans [11] "The sufferings of the present time are not worthy [to be compared] to the glory that is to be revealed in us". And even more forcefully: [12] "The things that were gain to me, these I have considered loss, on account of Christ. But I therefore consider all things loss, on account of the outstanding knowledge of Christ Jesus my Lord, for whom I have taken the loss of all things, and I consider them as dung." So on the absolute scale, creatures are triply good; yet on the relative scale, they are mere dung, compared to the glory that is to come.

To see this truth requires faith. It is quite the opposite of what our senses tell us. They insist that the things of this world alone are worthwhile.

So if we want our faith to grow, we need to *act on it,* to act according to it. That means, to actually part with some creatures and pleasures, and to be detached from the others, as Paul urged the Corinthians: [13] "The time is short. As for the rest, [I urge] that those who have wives be as though not having them, and those who weep, as though not weeping, and those who rejoice as though not rejoicing, and those who buy, as though not having, and those who use the world, as though not using it."

Another great reason why there is important spiritual value in giving up creatures and in mortification appears in the doctrinal introduction to a new document on indulgences by Pope Paul VI. Scholastic theologians had long taught that there is a universal moral order. We might compare it to the type of scales in which there are two pans, hung from a beam, which ought to balance. When someone sins, he as it were, takes for himself more than he should have: the scale is out of balance. Reparation for sin calls for putting the scales back into balance. That is done if the sinner himself, or someone acting for him, gives up something he otherwise might have legitimately had, or suffers some evil voluntarily. God, in His love of goodness, wants the scales balanced.

This new document of Paul VI marks the first time that the Magisterium of the Church has explicitly endorsed the theological teaching we have just sketched. The Pope said that [14] "for the full remission and reparation of sins, it is necessary that all the values of the universal moral order itself... be fully reestablished." He explains the Redemption in terms of this balancing, for he says there is a "treasury of the Church... which is the infinite and inexhaustible price that the expiations and merits of Christ have before God, offered that all humanity might be liberated from sin..." So the chief work of balancing the scales was done by Christ. But we saw in our previous study of the price of Redemption that the Father willed that the Redemption be made as rich as possible, by joining the contribution of Mary to that of Christ. Similarly, in this matter of the balancing of the scales, which is simply another aspect of the Redemption, Mary contributes: [15] "Furthermore, there pertain to this treasury also the truly immense, immeasurable, and ever new price that the prayers and good works of the Blessed Virgin Mary and all the Saints have before God." We note the Pope mentions the other Saints as well as Mary: it is the will of the Father that the balancing reparation be made not only by Christ the Head, but by the whole Christ, Head and Members. In the objective phase of the Redemption, there was only Christ and His Mother; in the subjective phase, the contribution of all the members of Christ is added.

So it is obvious: to imitate Mary and her Divine Son, we must take part in this work of reparation, of balancing the moral order. Such is the will of the Father. This cannot be done by giving up nothing, as the New Spirituality suggests.

Pope John XXIII wrote an almost frightening passage about the special duty of priests to join in this work.

In his Encyclical on the Cure of Ars, he quoted the Cure. [16] "His reply is well known to a priest who complained that his apostolic zeal was devoid of fruit: 'You have prayed humbly to God, you have wept, you have groaned, you have sighed. Did you add also fasting, staying awake, sleeping on the floor, chastisement of the body? As long as you have not come to these things, do not think you have tried everything.' Our mind turns again to priests who have the care of souls, and we beg them earnestly, to hear the vehement force of these words. Let each one, led by that supernatural prudence to which all our acts must be conformed, think over again his way of life, (and ask himself) whether it is such as the care of the people entrusted to him calls for."

NOTES

1. On the Church § 46.

2. Cf. Rom. 8,29; 8,17; 8,9.

3. In: **Pastoral Life,** Dec. 1967.

4. Note 19 on p. 497 on the Decree on Lay Apostolate § 7.

5. On Lay Apostolate § 7.

6. On the Church § 46.

7. On Missions § 5.

8. 2 Cor. 11,23-30.

9. Lk. 8,14.

10. Mt. 19,29.

11. Rom. 8,18.

12. Phil. 3,7-8.

13. 1 Cor. 7,29-31.

14. Paul VI, **Indulgentiarum doctrina.** AAS 59,5-7.

15. **Ibid.** 11-12.

16. John XXIII, **Sacerdotii nostri primordia,** August 1, 1959: AAS 51, 569.

11 — FOLLOWING AFTER THE CROSS WITH MARY

To mortify ourselves in imitation of Mary and her Divine Son brings many benefits. We have seen mortification as acting on faith so as to dispose ourselves to receive an increase of faith; we have seen it as atonement.

Now we want to examine a special aspect of mortification in relation to faith. That will help us gain some practical insights on the best ways to practice mortification.

Faith, as we know, is the total adherence of a man to God—in his mind, by assent to God's truth and by confident belief that God will keep His promises; in his will, by obeying the will of God.

It is this last aspect that interests us now: faith obeying God's will. Really, all spiritual perfection lies precisely in this. Why? There is only one thing in man that is free: the will. Our mind could be compared to a meter which ought merely to register the truth that stands before it. If only the mind sees clearly, it is dominated by the truth. Of course, there is such a thing as wishful thinking, in which our feelings or desires sway, even distort the reading of that mental meter.

Now, since only our will is free, if we take the only free element in us, and align it absolutely, in every respect, with the will of God, obviously there is nothing more that can be done: that is absolute perfection.

To understand just how we can align our wills with the will of God, we need to notice that there are, basically, two kinds of situations, one in which the will of God is already clearly known to us, the other, in which His will is, at least in some aspects, not yet clear.

The will of God becomes entirely clear to us when we are given a command by some lawful authority. Vatican II, as we saw in chapter 9, made clear to us that we must obey the authorities of the Church. St. Paul, writing to the Romans, even at the time when they were ruled by the unfortunate Emperor Nero, told them: [1] "Let every person be subject to superior authorities. For there is no authority except from God. Those that are in authority are put in place by God. So he who resists the authority, resists the ordinance of God."

It is sometimes said: The will of the superior is the will of God. This is true in one sense, false in another. It is true in the sense that God does want us to obey authorities, unless, of course, they order what is morally wrong. It is not however true in another sense, that is, it does not mean that what the superior decides is always the best. It may actually fall far short of the best, it may even be imprudent. Yet, unless it is morally wrong, we should obey. We recall the vehement words of Christ Himself about the Scribes and Pharisees. They were guilty of dreadful hypocrisy, as He Himself said. Yet He also said: [2] "The Scribes and Pharisees have taken their seat upon the seat of Moses," that is, they have religious authority. "Therefore, all things they say to you, do and observe. But do not do as they do."

But we have already examined this matter of obedience in chapter 9. Now we are concerned with another type of situation in which the will of God is clear: that of providentially sent difficulties. We all have them, they vary much in each individual life. Some of these difficulties are relatively small, such as the problem of being patient with other drivers in crowded traffic, or submitting to an irritable boss at work, or dealing with unreasonable customers in a store. Students may have to endure boring teachers; teachers, dull, unresponsive students; assembly line workers submit to a monotony more fitted for machines than for men. But there are more demanding trials: severe and prolonged sickness, loss of a limb or of sight or hearing, the death of loved ones, and even, open persecution for having done what is right, a persecution that sometimes comes from those who have a positive obligation to promote the cause of Christ. St. Paul told Timothy: [3] "All who want to live religiously in Christ Jesus will be persecuted." His words are all too true, even in our times.

How can we make the greatest spiritual profit from these things that are sent to us, or at least, permitted to come, by the hand of our Father? It is obvious that we should not grumble and complain, and here, we need to watch ourselves carefully. It is not too rare to see a devout person who will say: "I am completely resigned to the will of God. I will never complain." Yet, when difficulties do come, some of these persons complain more often and more bitterly than those who make no special profession of following religious ideals.

But we can and will go farther, if we want to make the greatest spiritual gain. We will not only not complain, we will positively welcome and embrace these difficulties, and be sincerely glad to have them. Of course, we do not mean to say that evil is not evil. St. Paul, as we saw, pictures the whole Christian life by saying that we are saved and made holy if and to the extent that we are not only members of Christ, but are like Him. Paul told the Romans that we are heirs with Christ [4] "if indeed we suffer with Him, so we may also be glorified with Him." Over this we rejoice, at the chance to be more like Christ, and His Mother. And St. Paul was right in adding: [5] "I judge that the sufferings of the present time are not worthy to be compared with the glory that is to be revealed in us." In the same vein, Christ Himself said: [6] "The servant is not greater than his master. If they persecuted me, they will persecute you," and: [7] "Blessed are you when they curse you and persecute you and say all evil against you, lying, for my sake. Be glad and exult, for your reward is copious in heaven."

At first sight, it may seem to be asking too much to suggest that we actually be glad over afflictions. And someone might even add: Did not He Himself suffer much, and even ask that the chalice pass from Him? Did not His Mother grieve most deeply at His passion? We make two points in reply. First, it is true, this is asking much. Yet, our human nature tends to follow the pattern of the pendulum: it swings readily from one extreme to another, but does not stop in the middle. Now one extreme is to complain over trials; the other is to accept them with joy. Precisely because they are at opposite ends of the scale, the action-reaction principle, the pendulum pattern, will help us, once we make the first bold break. Psychologists would add: It is the sign of a poorly adjusted person to indulge in flight from reality. To embrace it not only makes one well balanced, but makes the difficulties more easily bearable. It takes much of the sting out of them.

Secondly, we must admit that Mary and her Divine Son did grieve deeply and suffer bitterly. Yet this does not contradict what we have said. For there are many levels within a human being, from the vegetative and the animal levels up to the highest realms of the spirit. Suppose we think of a high mountain, whose peak pierces the clouds. On the lower slopes, as one looks up, he sees only blackness, clouds, storm. Yet on the peak itself all is clear: the sun is shining. Similarly, the lower levels of our nature may be most grievously afflicted; yet the point of the spirit, if we follow the way of Jesus and Mary, will rise up into unshakeable, ever-lasting serenity, peace, even joy.

When things are easy, and we enjoy consolation in the things of God, it is easy to adhere to His will. But when we must summon all our powers to hold on, then we are in a fortunate necessity. We must either make a large gain, by holding on tightly, or go down. So, we welcome the opportunity for a large gain in likeness to Christ and His Blessed Mother, by adhering to the Father's will strongly, in the dark, in spite of pressure to the contrary. The Father is more eager to give His graces than we are to receive them. If only we become more open, in this way, He can give more. That pleases Him the more, benefits us the more.

But not always are all aspects of the will of God clear. For example, a priest might be given an order to collect money for the relief of the poor. Since it is an order given by lawful authority, there is no doubt that God wills that the priest go ahead, and work diligently. But, to what extent God wills that the campaign succeed, by what means, what degree of progress, at what time: all these factors are not really clear. God for His own good reasons may wish to make it necessary to work harder, to delay results, to give success through means different from what our poor minds imagine should be the case. So we need to preserve a sort of pliability in working even for certainly good things. Or, to put it another way: there are two sides to such a picture, one in which God's will is clear, the other, in which it is not. Where His will is clear we should not be simply passive: we should actively will and work for what He wants, to the extent that His will is clear. But in the other aspect, that in which we do not know all details of His will, there we pre-serve a sort of expectant pliability, ready to actively align ourselves with His will when that becomes clear.

Again, God might seem to give a religious vocation to

some young person. That is of course a good thing. Yet He might wish to frustrate that, to send or permit instead some lingering illness that makes the carrying out of such a vocation impossible. Here too, we need to distinguish the two sides, and to align actively with the clear aspect of God's will, to hold ourselves in adaptive readiness for the later appearance of the features of His will that are not clear at the start.

If we are to be able to recognize God's will as it gradually unfolds in such cases as these—and in many less dramatic situations too, even in the small decisions of daily living—we need as it were some conditioning. That consists in mortifying our desires. [8] We might approach it this way. Our Lord told us: [9] "Where your treasure is, there is your heart also." Our treasure is anything that strongly attracts us, it is anything that exerts a pull on our thoughts, our wills, our inferior nature. We might compare it to a gravitational force, tending to pull everything towards itself. Some put their treasure in fine meals: when their minds are free, they love to daydream about eating; others put their treasure in powerful cars, or in accumulated wealth, or in travel, or in sex, or even in studying theology. Now all these things are legitimate, within proper bounds. But even if we think of only the legitimate use of these things, they still can create a danger for us. All of them are good, but they are less lofty, less good than God. Some of them are even more elevated than the common level: but as long as the level on which they lie is even somewhat lower than the level on which God is found, they can hinder our ascent. By pulling our thoughts, our desires, our hearts and sensitivities to a level that is anything less than the divine level, they make it that much less easy for us to rise.

Suppose, then, that God sends a grace, which is intended to lead me to do some good thing. But suppose also that I have within me a strong desire that goes in the opposite direction. The pull of that opposing force will make it hard for the pull of divine grace to have its effect, for divine grace is gentle, in that it respects our freedom.

It is clear, then, that our mortifications can do double or even multiple duty if we use them not only as a means to prepare for greater faith (by acting on faith), not only as a means of atonement (balancing the scales of the moral order) but also as a means of removing the pulls of creatures that make it less easy for us to discern the will of God in concrete, individual situations.

St. John of the Cross compares such pulls or attachments to a line that holds a bird down. [10] Suppose, he says a bird is tied down by a thick rope: it can fly no higher than the rope permits. But suppose instead of a rope, he is held only by a thread of the same length: as long as he does not break that thread, he is still limited to the same amount of rise. Similarly, it matters little, says St. John, whether it be a great or a large attachment that limits our ascent to God: so long as we do not break that thread, our flight is confined to the lower reaches. We can never reach perfection.

As we saw in chapter 10, we need both providential and self-imposed mortification. St. Paul, as we said, had a most unusual measure of, unsought, providentially permitted difficulties in the course of his missionary labours. Yet he imposed on himself also fasting and other penances. There seem to be two reasons: the total *amount* of penance was, in his opinion, not enough without these additions; and also self-imposed mortifications can be carefully directed precisely against those spots in our tendencies that need curbing the most.

How much self-imposed mortification is needed in the life of each person? No general rule can be given. We can only notice that we are very apt to go to extremes. Most persons go to the extreme of not doing enough; a few will go to the opposite extreme, and damage health, in their imprudence. The reason for both extremes is the fact that it is hard to be objective about one's own case, especially in matters of this kind. So, if possible, we do well to get the help of an experienced spiritual director, to help us choose general guidelines for mortification, and to make adjustments in those policies at intervals. How often such revision will be in order will of course vary much in individual cases.

Finally, we can not only imitate the total dedication of Mary to the will of God, by which she even consented to the dread immolation of her Divine Son; but we can also obtain another special help from her. We need to ask her to obtain light and strength for us. And there is still another service she will perform for us if we wish. In civil law it is possible to appoint an attorney to act in our name in certain matters. Now in this matter of trials and mortifications, we do not always know all aspects of the will of the Father. Especially, we do not know if it would please Him if we would *ask for* some trials or sufferings, to atone for our own sins or those of others. We would like to do more than just wait passively, in a pliant state, until His will appears. We would like to actively will what He wants. In the interval before His will becomes clear, we can make a closer approach to active alignment if we give to her a sort of Power of Attorney. That is, we appoint her to speak for us to the Father, to make in our name any offer of accepting any specific future trials which it might please Him to have us make. We do not know what to ask for: she does. She can raise our pliant expectancy to active alignment, for she will actively speak for us if we ask her to do it.

NOTES

1. Rom. 13,1-2.

2. Mt. 23,2-4.

3. 2 Tim. 3,12.

4. Rom. 8,17.

5. Rom. 8,18.

6. Jn. 15,20.

7. Mt. 5,11-12.

8. We know for certain that God wills His glory and our salvation. So we must surely desire these. But to what extent they are to be advanced, by what means, at what time, that is less certain. In all else, if we cultivate desires, we may not be in line with His will. St. John of the Cross, especially in the first book of his **Ascent of Mt. Carmel,** speaks eloquently of the importance of mortifying desires. His words are to be understood with the distinctions we have just outlined. Cf. also St. Francis de Sales, **Treatise on the Love of God,** Books 8,9 and 10:4-5.

9. Mt. 6,21.

10. **Ascent of Mt. Carmel** 1,11,4.

12 — GOD IS LOVE

At the beginning of an earlier chapter [1] we began to wonder why Vatican II places so much stress on the faith and obedience of Mary, why it spoke more of those virtues than it did of her love. We began to reply by examining, in the light of the Council, the importance of faith and obedience. But we still need to ask ourselves: granted that faith and obedience are basic, still, is not love the greatest of all virtues? Why not speak more of it?

To complete the answer, we need first to recall what love really is. Few ages have prated more of love than ours; yet few centuries have shown more confusion over its basic meaning. We often read or hear the expression "to make love" used to refer to sexual intercourse, as if that were love. And a prominent theologian showed an almost unbelievable confusion when he wrote that to explain the meaning of love, one has to describe some bodily activity. So, a difficulty arises, he says, when we speak of God as loving, since He has no body. As a result, he asserts, when we say God is loving, we take a word we understand in a bodily context, and extend it into a realm we do not understand. So really, we do not know what we mean when we say God is loving. We are just using words to try to mean something. [2]

St. John, the beloved disciple, wrote that "God *is* love." If a theologian does not know what that means, one wonders if he should call himself a theologian at all.

We can learn most easily what love is from the Beloved Disciple. In his Gospel, he quotes the Divine Teacher as saying: [3] "God so loved the world that He gave His Only-begotten Son, so that everyone who believes in Him may not perish, but may have eternal life." And again: [4] "By this has the love of God become known to us [namely] that God sent His Only-begotten into the world, that we might live through Him."

So, God showed His love by sending His Son to die to obtain eternal happiness for us. What then is the *interior attitude,* which leads to that *exterior effect,* His sending His Son to obtain happiness for us? Obviously, it must be this: He desires, wants our happiness. Not just a merely human, passing happiness, but an everlasting happiness, a divine sort of happiness. So then we can easily see what love is: It is a desire, a concern for the happiness and the well-being of another. Because God desires our happiness, He sent His Son.

How great is that love? We can as it were get a measure on love by seeing how great an obstacle it can surmount in its attempt to obtain happiness for the loved one. A small love will stop short when it meets a small obstacle; a great love can be blocked by a great obstacle. A limitless love will not hold back no matter what the cost. What was the cost of opening the way to eternal, divine happiness for us? It was the hard life, the dread passion and death of the Divine Son. The very difficulty of it is the measure of the love of both Father and Son for us.

How great was Mary's love for us? It too was measured by the suffering she had to go through to cooperate in obtaining eternal happiness for us. It meant, as Vatican II said that: [5] "she stood, in accord with the divine plan, greatly grieved with her Only-begotten, and joined herself to His sacrifice with a Motherly heart, consenting to the immolation of the victim that had been born of her." How difficult was this for her? The pain of any Mother standing helplessly by as her son dies would be in proportion to two things: to the suffering she sees him going through, and the greatness of her love for him. The more she loves him, the greater the pain. Each new degree, as it were, of love, multiplies the suffering she feels from the extent of his pains. Her love is as it were a multiplier.

How great was her love for Him? Since love of God and holiness are, in practice, interchangeable expressions, we get a clue from the words that Pius IX wrote referring to her holiness at the time of her immaculate conception. Even then, at the start, it was so great that [6] "none greater under God can be thought of, and no one but God can comprehend it." Now of course, her holiness or love grew after that start—we all must either grow or fall back. What then must it have been by the time of His sacrifice, if at the very start it was beyond the ability of any creature to understand, if only God Himself could comprehend it? Let that incomprehensible love be the multiplier of the suffering endured from seeing His terrible physical pain and most heartless rejection by the very men He was dying to save, and if we could begin to take in such a height or depth, we could begin to understand the immensity of the obstacle her love had to surmount in order to cooperate with Him in obtaining happiness, eternal joy, for us.

So her love for us is, quite literally, beyond the ability of any creature to measure.

But there is still a most difficult problem. We have seen that love is a desire or a concern for the happiness and well-being of another person. We want that person to receive what he needs in order to be well off and happy. Now of course there is no problem if we say that God wishes us to receive what we need for happiness, or if we wish such a thing to another human being. But: can we really, as it were, turn to God and say: "I hope you are well-off. I wish you all the things you need for happiness." Obviously, God cannot be other than infinitely well off. He needs nothing. We creatures can give Him nothing. We speak of "serving God." But really: does our "service" benefit Him? The Book of Job replies: [7] "If you sin, what harm do you do Him? . . . If you are morally righteous, what do you give Him, or what does He receive from your hand?"

In what sense, then, can we say at all that we love God? We must notice that often words are used to apply to two things in such a way that they apply somewhat differently in the two cases: there is something in common in the two uses, but also something different. Similarly, when we say we love God, we must use the word "love" in a sense that is partly the same, partly different. We can understand it this way: Scripture pictures God as pleased when we obey, displeased when we disobey. Now of course, He is not pleased in that He gains anything from our "service." We have already seen that. But yet He, like a good Father, is pleased for two reasons. An earthly father wants his children to obey, first, because he loves what is right, and moral rightness does require that a child obey his parents; second, because he, the father, wants to give his love and favours to his child. But if the child is bad, the father really ought to punish instead. That he does not want. Similarly with our Father in heaven. He wants us to obey because He loves what is morally right: it is right that children obey their parents, creatures their Creator. But He too wants to give us happiness, to lavish His gifts upon us. If we disobey, He must punish instead. He does not want that. So He is, in this sense, pleased when we obey, not that He gains, but so that He may have the pleasure of giving.

When we obey, we make it possible for Him to give. That gives Him pleasure. So that is what it means to love

Him: to obey Him, so we may be open to His gifts, so He may have the pleasure of giving to us. In this sense, we make Him happy.

We can now understand some otherwise puzzling lines in Scripture. Christ Himself said: [8] "He who has my commandments and keeps them, he it is who loves me." And again: [9] "If you love me, keep my commandments." The second Epistle of St. John puts it even more concisely: [10] "This is love [namely] that we walk according to His commands."

No wonder then, that Vatican II spoke more often of Mary's obedience than of her love, and that it said of her Son, [11] "By His obedience, He brought about Redemption." Of course, there is a formal distinction between obedience and love. Yet in practice, they are almost indistinguishable, surely inseparable. We could put it well by saying: Obedience is love in action.

When is love perfect? We saw in chapter 11 that absolute perfection consists in totally aligning our will with the will of God, so that we actively will what He wills, wherever and to whatever extent His will is known to us, and we wait in docile, pliable expectancy for His will to appear in other matters. Really, that is simply another description of love, for love of God, as we saw, consists in making ourselves totally open to Him by obedience to His will, so He may have the pleasure of lavishing His generosity on us. We saw too, that an important aspect in aligning our will with His lies in our working to mortify desires. For these can prevent us from seeing His will fully.

To put it another way, perfect love requires that we not only avoid all mortal sin, but even that we avoid all deliberate venial sin, and further, that we eradicate all attachments that are imperfect, to the extent that they could hinder our most fully seeing the will of God. For even an imperfection, that is, doing something less perfect than we could do, or omitting some good we could do can hinder our ascent, much like the thread holding the bird, of which we spoke in chapter 11. Now we do not mean, of course, that a man should, on the *objective scale,* always do that which is the most perfect thing he can conceive at the moment. No, considering normal human weakness, as found in *this* person at *this* moment, what is *better in itself* might not be the *better thing for him* at this point. In fact, we need to add that for most persons, a constant policy of trying to find even the best for themselves on this occasion requires an expenditure of energy that, if sustained over a long period, would probably be too much, would probably be contrary to prudence.

Of course, there will be many variations in what is prudent for *this* person according to his state in life, e.g., no husband should impose anything resembling a monastic regime on his family, nor is he personally called to live like a monk.

In practice, two measures are needed to help us find our way, to achieve just the right measure and balance. First, we need mortification, chiefly mortification of desires, so that their gravitational force (recall chapter 11) may not be able to hinder the ascent of our minds, wills, hearts to God. This mortification itself too, of course, is equally and for the same reason, to be regulated by supernatural prudence, which must take into account the reservations and distinctions expressed in the last paragraph above. Really, if at all possible, one should have the help of a prudent spiritual director in setting policies on this matter, and in making periodical reviews of those policies. For no one can be objective about himself.

Secondly, we need the help and guidance that our spiritual Mother Mary can and will obtain for us. But even with that, we should not forget that we are not infallible, that we can, even without intending to do so, block the light she sends us because of desires that exert their pull on us subconsciously.

We can speak of varied degrees of perfection in love of God also according to the *kind of motive* we have. That is, we can love God because He is *good in Himself*, or because He is *good to or for us*. *Objectively*, of course, He is both, and we know that if we love Him as good in Himself, He will also reward us. But there can be a difference of emphasis, of the way one or the other aspect registers on us at a given moment. We should try to make the more generous aspect the more prominent. If we understand what was said earlier in this chapter about the generosity of God, about the fact that He wants us to "serve" Him not for any gain to Himself, which is impossible, but so He may give His favours to us, we will find that almost the more natural thing to do.

We should notice too that when we speak of love of God because He is *good to or for us,* we could have two different aspects in mind. That is, we could either desire Him in such a way that we think of *union with Him* as what we want, or that we think of *the joy He gives* as our goal. Again, both are inseparable in reality. It is a question of which aspect dominates in our thoughts at a given moment.

Some persons, aiming at the most refined love, have thought that fear of divine punishment is an unworthy motive, one to be avoided. It is true, fear is a much lower motive than love. But that does not mean it is a bad motive. Christ Himself often presented that motive to His disciples. In fact, the first clear revelation of hell in Scripture is not found in the Old Testament, but on the lips of Christ Himself. It would be far better if we could always be driven only by the purest motives of love. But, considering our weakness, and the blinding force of human emotions, there will be times when love does not register strongly on us, when we need the help of fear to keep from falling out of His love.

Some may be tempted to say at this point: But I did not enter a monastery or a religious order. I am not aiming at perfection. There are two things to be said in reply. First, everything said about mortification, perfection, love, and other things, must be adjusted to the special individual characteristics of each person, to his present stage of spiritual development, and to his particular state in life. What is proper for a monk or hermit will not always be proper for a married person. But, secondly, with these reservations, perfection definitely is not only open to all, but all are required to work towards it. The Divine Teacher Himself said: [12] "Be you therefore perfect, as your Father in Heaven is perfect." Obviously, no creature can ever actually attain the perfection of the Father in Heaven. The result is that he can never say it is enough. He must always keep on the move, always grow. [13]

NOTES

1. In chapter 8.

2. As a matter of charity, we omit his name. And of course, it is just possible he may have meant a sense somewhat different.

3. Jn. 3,16.

4. 1 Jn. 4,9.

5. On the Church § 58.

6. **Ineffabilis Deus,** Dec. 8, 1854.

7. Job 35,6-7.

8. Jn. 14,21.

9. Jn. 14,15.

10. 2 Jn. 6.

11. On the Church § 3.

12. Mt. 5, 48.

13. The obligation to work towards perfection is more stringent on religious than on lay persons, and still more so on priests.

13 — LOVE FOR ALL SONS OF MARY

Love, we have seen, is a desire, a concern for the happiness and well-being of another. God's love for us is His desire for our eternal happiness. This was no mere empty wish on His part. As St. Paul told the Romans, [1] "God *proved* His love for us, because when we were still sinners, Christ died for us." We love God if we give Him the pleasure of being able to lavish His favours on us. We do this by aligning ourselves totally with His will, by obedience and conformity in all things. That makes us open, capable of receiving His gifts: then He can give, and He loves to give.

Obviously, if we want to have Him have this supremely generous pleasure, we will want also other human beings to be similarly open, so He may have the pleasure of giving to them, so they will obtain eternal happiness. But that is what is meant by love of neighbour: wanting his eternal happiness.

We can see now how inextricably intertwined are love of God and love of neighbour. We cannot wish Him the fulness of His generous happiness in giving, without wishing that our neighbour be open to Him by obedience to His will. But when our neighbour is so disposed, he is also by that very fact going to receive eternal happiness. So when we wish for either thing—either that God may have the pleasure of giving, or that others may receive—we inescapably wish for both. No wonder then that the Divine Teacher told us that the second commandment is like to the first. We cannot love God without loving neighbour.

Mary our Mother is the Mother of all men, since she shared in earning all graces for all men, and, as Vatican II put it "as a result" of this sharing in the Redemption "she is our Mother in the order of grace." We have already dwelt on how dearly it cost her to become our spiritual Mother: it meant consenting to the death of her Only-begotten. As we saw in chapter 12, that suffering of hers, being measured by an immeasurable love of her Son, was literally beyond our ability to measure. Her love for us, while not so great, of course, as that for her Son and God, was yet in proportion to it, and so, being in proportion to something immeasurable, must be itself beyond measure.

Now if we really love our neighbour, we will be concerned about *everything* essential that he needs for his happiness. If someone desires only *some* of the essentials for another's happiness, but leaves out other necessary things, then we must suspect that whatever is motivating him, it cannot be love. For if it were love, it would take in everything.

It is at this point that so many persons make serious mistakes today. For example, those who propose "Situation Ethics" say that there is only one absolute principle in moral matters: love. Now that happens to be true, for all perfection is summed up in the twofold command of love of God and love of neighbour. Love is the fulfilment of the law. But, sadly, those who follow Situation Ethics do not really understand love, and so are not able to deduce, as it were, from this broad principle, all the things that really follow from it. For example, if we ask a practitioner of Situation Ethics: [2] "Is adultery wrong?" he will reply: "I don't know. Give me a case." He thinks that in some cases adultery is right, in some cases not. Thereby he betrays himself as not knowing what love really is. For St. Paul, writing under divine inspiration, warned us: [3] "Do not deceive yourselves. Neither the sexually immoral, nor idolaters, nor adulterers ... will inherit the kingdom of God." Now if they do not inherit the kingdom of God, they will be eternally unhappy. To tell others that adultery is right at least sometimes, is to lead them into doing something that will result in eternal *un*happiness, unless of course, they are excused by ignorance. But those who give such teaching, prove they do not know what love really is.

Again, others will be most zealous for neighbour in promoting civil rights. That of course, if done correctly, is not only permitted but highly praiseworthy, and even, to a certain extent, required. But when they see their neighbour exposed to pornography which entails the risk of forfeiting the only happiness that really matters, that which is divine and everlasting, the same persons sometimes do not care. Or they even defend pornography. They too do not understand love.

Many confuse love with emotion or feeling. It is easy to see that love is not really a feeling. We saw that in chapter 12 when we learned from the example of God Himself that love is really something much deeper, something that lies in the spirit. It is a desire or concern for the happiness and well-being of another.

We can see the same thing in another way. We recall that Christ commanded us to love our neighbour, and that He made clear that everyone is my neighbour. Suppose we become very concrete and specific about it. We think of the people who live on the corner, three blocks from here. Do we at this moment have a warm *feeling,* or any kind of a *feeling* toward them? It is rather likely we do not even know the name of those people. Similarly for all the people who live far from us, in other parts of this nation or of the world: it is simply impossible to have *feelings* towards them at all times. Yet Christ commands love. The implication is easy to see: He does not give impossible commands. But He would be ordering the impossible if He told us to have warm feelings towards every person on the globe. So, love must not be a feeling. It must not even have to include a feeling, for that would be just as impossible.

In fact, He commands us to love even our enemies. Suppose we think of some specific enemy, perhaps one of the Communist tyrants. Do we now have a warm feeling towards him? The same conclusion follows in the same way: Love is not a feeling, doesn't even have to include a feeling.

How then do we love all men? Very simply, we merely carry out what we have already said: We desire for them eternal happiness, and happiness here too, especially that happiness that is a means leading to the lasting happiness. We not only desire their happiness, we do something about it too. That means most of all that we pray for their welfare, eternal and temporal. And, according to our means, state of life, and opportunities, we try to lead them to eternal happiness by teaching them the eternal truths, by giving them good example, by helping protect them against moral dangers. Nor should we neglect—again, according to our means, state of life, and opportunities—to be concerned about the material welfare of those in need. We do this both as individuals, and as members of society, or of nations. Again, according to our means and their needs.

Sometimes good persons are worried, and even accuse themselves of hating someone, because they have an irrational feeling of aversion towards a certain person. At times, if questioned, they can point to a specific reason for that temptation to aversion or dislike; at other times, and this is even more common, they cannot give a reason. Such aversions are, as we said, irrational. We need to recognize that they are, at the start, just temptations. They become sin only if we go along with them, indulge in them deliberately and freely. Sometimes in spite of our best, most honest efforts, such irrational temptations continue. It is important to recognize them as temptations. For if we think we have sinned, when we really have not, then out of discouragement we may give up and *really* sin.

How to deal with such irrational aversions? At very least, we must not deliberately indulge them. And we should make it a special point to pray for the happiness, eternal and temporal, of the persons towards whom we have such feelings. Such prayer is true love. As long as we continue that, we cannot simultaneously hate. Of course, we need to watch out for possible self-deception here. Someone might say: "I am praying for that person", and then, feeling secure, might indulge in feelings of hatred really and deliberately. In many cases it is good to act very directly contrary to the aversion, by going out of our way to be pleasant to such a person. Not infrequently we will find out after a while that he or she is really a very enjoyable person, we just had never tried. Of course, sometimes it will be otherwise. In some cases it is impossible to arrive at such a result. At least, we can then sincerely and honestly pray for the other, and avoid any deliberate indulgence in the feelings of dislike. [4]

One of the commonest failures in charity is detraction, that is, making known hidden faults of another without a proportionate reason. To reveal such faults is harmful to another's reputation, to which he or she has a right. So the sin is not only uncharity, it is injustice as well. There are times when there is a proportionate reason for revealing faults of another. But we ought to recognize that we are all too naturally prone to overestimate the reasons. We will, if we are realistic, make allowance for that tendency in making our decision before speaking.

There is a kind of venial sin which theologians used to call "affection to venial sin". The term is not too clear. What it really means is this: If I have an affection to a particular venial sin, I have as it were a gap or hole in my intention to do good and to refrain from sin. It is as if I said to myself: "I do not intend to commit every kind of sin. But I am making a reservation or two for myself. I do not intend to make a business of knifing my neighbour in the back with my tongue regularly. But there are times when I do enjoy it, when it is hard to keep a conversation going without telling the latest I know about someone's secret faults. In such situations, I am going to keep on doing it."

Such an attitude is literally devastating to the spiritual development of the one who has it. Really, he cannot make any progress at all. The reason is simple. He by this very policy sets a low limit for himself. Or, he as it were puts a clamp around his heart, saying: "I will not open my heart to God's will in this respect." As long as the clamp is on, one's heart cannot enlarge to the point of greater love of God or neighbour. And if that be the case, there is *no progress*. It is sad to see some who work well, apparently, on their spiritual growth in other respects, yet cancel it all out by such an affection to the venial sin of detraction.

Of course, there can be an affection to any kind of venial sin. Holding on in the same way to any kind of sin equally blocks all spiritual growth.

St. Paul warned the Corinthians that sometimes [5] "Satan himself transforms himself into an angel of light." He means that he acts as though he were one, to further some evil purpose. That is happening today in this matter of love of neighbour. Some today, led by the false angel of light, so exalt love of neighbour as to almost wipe out love of God. One priest I know, said: "If I were alone on a desert island, I could have no relation to God, for I can have that only through people." The error is in supposing that love of neighbour is *identified* with love of God. The two are *inseparable,* as we have seen, but they are *not identical.* We do love God when we make ourselves personally open to His will, as we have seen, so He may have the generous pleasure of lavishing His gifts on us. That is a direct relation to God, which does not go through love of neighbour, even though both attitudes are inseparable. So many are deceiving themselves, being deceived by the false angel of light, and are neglecting the First and the Great Commandment on pretext that the Second—which is *like* to the First, but not the *same*—alone suffices. The plot is truly diabolical, for many fear to speak out against what appears to be love of neighbour, knowing well that such love is essential. Such persons are apt to turn love into mere do-goodism, or even into mere philanthropy. Such things, properly cultivated, can be good. But we must not neglect direct love of God, which can lead even to the intense, almost tangible contact with God that comes in infused contemplation, which we will discuss in a later chapter.

Mary knew how to love all of us, her spiritual children. But she did not for one moment think that love of us was her only relation to God, who was her Son.

NOTES

1. Rom. 5,8.

2. Cf. Joseph Fletcher, **Situation Ethics,** (Westminster, Philadelphia, 1966) 142,164-65,74.

3. 1 Cor. 6,9.

4. It is particularly important to avoid the mistake, not infrequent among otherwise good people, of refusing to speak to another for long periods.

5. 2 Cor. 11,14.

14 — FEELINGS AND LOVE

Now that we know that full spiritual development consists in perfect love, or, to put it another way, in the absolute alignment of our wills with the will of God, we can easily see what to think about emotions or feelings in religious matters. Emotions are not love, as we know. So, they will be useful or harmful according as they tend to promote love, or to hinder it. They can do either thing, on varied occasions.

Since emotions or feelings are capable of being used well or badly, we can easily guess that they may originate in different ways, that is, some may come from God, aimed at good; others may come from the evil spirits, designed to lead us to evil. And some can come even from variations in merely natural conditions.

Emotions, or a feeling of satisfaction in religious matters, are often called *consolations*. The reverse, a lack of feeling and of satisfaction, is often called *dryness*.

God quite commonly sends consolations in spiritual things to those who are just beginning to break with attachments to earthly things, to encourage them to turn their eyes more to the things above. Such consolations obviously can be quite helpful. But there are dangers. The Evil One may try to persuade such persons that now that they are experiencing emotions over spiritual goods they must be well advanced in the spiritual life, that perhaps they are beginning to be Saints. Probably the most devastating of all vices is spiritual pride. If the devil can lead a person into it, he can turn all attempts at spiritual growth into poison. For this reason the devil himself sometimes stirs up emotions to induce a person to want to pray more, to do more good things. The Evil One can well afford it, if he simultaneously leads the same one into spiritual pride. He has other tricks too. For example, he can lead someone into making overly ambitious resolutions for spiritual growth. Precisely because the man takes on too much, he will inevitably fall, and will be likely to give up future attempts.

But even if none of these things happen to one from consolations, there is a more subtle danger. St. Francis de Sales puts it well when he says [1] that we could be led to love the consolations of God instead of the God of consolations. That is, our real stimulus to do what is spiritually good may be not purely love of God, but the pleasure we get from it. We have already seen that true perfection is the alignment of our wills with the will of God. We know too that faith, which is the total adherence of a man to God, grows strongest when it must work in the dark, holding on when that seems humanly impossible. So we can now see equally that when we stand firm and try our best to please God in spite of dryness, the lack of any feeling, that we may be pleasing Him far more than when all seems to go smoothly. A prayer, such as the Rosary, said with abundant distractions can be priceless. As long as we do our best to eject the distractions *every time we notice them,* we are exerting our wills to match the will of God, and we are doing it vigorously. We added the qualification "every time we notice them", because it is very possible for a sincere person to be swept along for considerable periods by distractions, so engrossed in them that he does not realize he is distracted. But if when, as it were, he comes to himself, he takes action, then he is growing spiritually.

We can see too what to think of the plea of many persons today that they have stopped going to Mass because it is not meaningful, it is irrelevant. They really mean: "I do not get any satisfaction out of it, so it is no good for me." The Evil One has really triumphed if he leads a man to say that the center of all grace is meaningless! He has compounded his victory by leading many into celebrating the renewal [2] of the obedience of Christ by disobedience to the Church, on the grounds that they *feel* the liturgy is not meaningful unless they indulge in unending tinkering, constantly chasing an ever-receding rainbow of personal satisfaction, instead of simply trying to please God.

Of course Satan can inject a twist of another kind into dryness. He can lead a soul to be proud, to say: "Weaker souls need consolations, but *I* am strong!"

Sometimes too whether or not we experience emotion or feelings of satisfaction can be affected by merely natural conditions. If we are overly tired, internally sluggish, or even suffering from poor digestion, we will be less likely to have consolations. Is it true then that good vibrant health promotes consolations? Not necessarily. When this life is most pleasant, the things of eternity may seem less real to us. Further, in illness and other trials we are apt to meet with a higher kind of consolation. As we saw in chapter 11, since we human beings are made up of matter and spirit, with many levels, drives, and needs in each part, we can be in consolation on the highest level, while we are suffering on the lower levels. As such, we can be like a mountain so lofty that it pierces the clouds, on whose lower slopes, there is blackness and storm; while on the peak, the sun is always shining. We can be sure that even in the darkness of Calvary our Blessed Mother and her Son had this higher light, while at the same time, they suffered most bitterly.

Some say that emotion plays a considerable role in a new movement, called Pentecostalism, in which many claim to have received the gifts of tongues, of healing, of prophecy, after a special Baptism in the Spirit. In the first century of the Church such gifts were quite common. On the first Pentecost, when the apostles were assembled with Mary the Mother of Jesus, the Spirit came upon all in the form of fiery tongues, and they began to speak in various languages, so that Jews then visiting in Jerusalem for the great feast each understood them speaking in his own native tongue. Somewhat later, St. Paul, in his first letter to Corinth, devotes three chapters [3] to gifts that may have been of the same sort as those recorded on the first Pentecost. However, St. Paul makes several distinctions. First, he points out that not every seeming instance of such gifts is really from the good Spirit: some are from the Evil One. [4] He goes on to speak of the relative value of the gifts. Tongues is the least of them, to be used in Church services only if there is someone who can translate: [5] otherwise, the one having such a gift is to be silent. Prophecy, he says, is to be more highly regarded, for it is the gift of giving a moving exhortation to the community (the word as St. Paul uses it need not imply ability to foretell the future). But then, at the end of chapter 12 and the start of the beautiful chapter 13, Paul advises the Corinthians: "Be eager for the better gifts. And now I show you the way par excellence! If I speak with the tongues of men and of angels, yet do not have love, I have become a noisy gong or a clanging cymbal." The reason is that there are two categories of graces. The first is that sort of grace which makes one holy by the very fact that he has it. Included in this first class is love of God and neighbour, or, what is inseparable from them, sanctifying grace. Actual graces, which God sends to lead us to do His will are closely allied to this first group. The second group, charismatic graces, consists of those favours which do *not* automatically make the recipient holy: they are aimed at other ends, at special benefits for the Church: [6]

"First, apostles, second, prophets, third, teachers, then, wonder-workers, then, gifts of healing, helpers of the poor, administrators, kinds of tongues." We note that St. Paul puts the grace of apostleship first, that of tongues last. Apostolic graces do not seem miraculous or extraordinary, as tongues do, yet they are more important for the Church. Paul fears his friends are being childish about tongues: [7] "Brothers, don't be children mentally, but be children in regard to malice." He wants them to put chief emphasis on love and union with God. The charismatic gifts are desirable and good, but not to be compared with the graces that automatically make men holy.

These gifts became rare in the mainline church after the first century. From then on, it was only heretical sects that claimed to have them in profusion. Of course, that does not mean today's Pentecostals are heretical. But neither has it been proved just which spirit is at work in each case.

We say "in each case" since each instance needs to be evaluated separately. Many Pentecostals seem content to say that the manifestations match the description given by St. Paul: therefore they are from the good Spirit. But we need evidence that these things are *really* the same, not just apparently the same. They then plead: by their fruits you shall know them. Pentecostalism, they say, leads men to greater love of God, charity to neighbour, love of Scripture, and to many other good things. So, they assert, we are not just placing stress on charismatic favours to the detriment of the main line things.

These things, again, seem true, but need further examination. For the Evil One could well afford to promote some apparent good, even to tolerate some real good, for some times, as long as he would gain in the long run. Now, as we said, not all cases of Pentecostalism today are the same. Some leave room for suspicion: even though certain persons do seem to bear fine spiritual fruits, yet the same ones give up the basic principles of religious life, following instead the new spirituality. [8] One can afford to be cautious over such cases. Others, however, show no such deviation. In fact, some explicitly reject the new spirituality, and follow all, not just some, of the solid rules of the spiritual life. Some are persons who before entering the Pentecostal movement had almost given up the practice of their faith. Of such cases we may ask: in the first century, God gave such gifts to help establish the faith for the first time; perhaps now He judges the use of the same gifts needed to restore lost faith in an age in which faith is decaying?

At least we can be certain of this: all Pentecostals have special reason to carefully apply the principles we have reviewed on the right use of emotion in religion.

Did Mary have the Pentecostal gifts, or consolations? We know from the Acts of the Apostles that she was in the group upon whom the Holy Spirit descended in the form of fiery tongues. As to consolations, we can only surmise. Some, such as St. Therese of Lisieux, [9] have liked to think she enjoyed but little of such favours, that she always walked in the darkness of faith. Others have thought that since she was so specially favoured by God in other ways, she must have had these favours too. Of course, the argument does not hold: feelings, as we have seen, can be helpful, but can also be harmful. It all depends on our use of them. We can only be sure that hers was a magnificent faith, that on the occasions of the greatest mysteries of her Son had to hold on strongly in the dark. Whether or not she enjoyed pleasurable feelings at other times, we simply do not know, other than that, as we said, in the "peak of the soul", she must have had that higher form of peace and consolation which no storm could ever destroy.

NOTES

1. **Introduction to a Devout Life** 4,13.

2. Cf. Vatican II, On the Liturgy § 10.

3. 1 Cor. Chapters 12-14

4. 1 Cor. 12,1-3.

5. 1 Cor. 14,28.

6. 1 Cor. 12,28.

7. 1 Cor. 14,20.

8. Cf. Chap. 10 above.

9. She liked to think that Mary had walked the path of dryness, with no special manifestations. Cf. **Novissima Verba: The Last Confidences of St. Therese** (Kenedy, N. Y., 1952) pp. 109-11.

15 — LOVE OF LOWLINESS

"The Father of Mercies willed that the acceptance of the predestined Mother should come before the Incarnation, so that in this way, just as a woman contributed to death, so also a woman should contribute to life." [1] Vatican II thus describes the day of the Annunciation. Mary was [2] "not just employed by God in a passive way, but ... she cooperated in human salvation by free faith and obedience." In spite of the doubts of some modern theologians, she must have known at least something of that to which she was consenting. Otherwise she would be largely passive, not free. But even if we were to accept the view [3] that she knew only that He was to be the promised Messiah, without knowing of His Divinity, we still must stand amazed at this: Why did she not run quickly to the Jewish priests and exultantly tell them: "I feel it my duty to report to you that the one whom the prophets have so long foretold is now at hand. An Archangel appeared to me. I have conceived without the intervention of man. The Messiah is to be my son."

Of course, she did nothing of the kind. She did not even reveal her great secret to St. Joseph, she did not even speak to defend herself against the otherwise very plausible charge of adultery.

The later events of her life are of the same tone. She never sought for, never gained recognition for herself. When her Son was triumphantly offered Kingship by the crowds, there is no mention of her. But she did step forth from the shadows of modest retirement into the deep blackness of

Calvary, after the Apostles, the sharers in His acclaim, had fled. She willingly took part in His disgrace, His shame, His rejection.

She not only did not seek recognition: she gladly accepted non-recognition, even disgrace. Why?

As we saw in chapter 8, she was accustomed to the darkness of faith, in which she often had to hold to two things· that, humanly speaking, seemed impossible. On the one hand, she knew at least something of her own dignity, at least as the Mother of the Messiah. Probably she knew also that she was the Mother of God. Of that surpassing pinnacle Pius XI wrote that it is a [4] "dignity second only to God" and he goes on to call it "a sort of infinite dignity, from the infinite good that God is." Yet, simultaneously, she considered and knew that she was nothing.

How reconcile these two things? Theologians love to speculate on such problems, and to dwell on them in a devout way is very profitable. No doubt she whom St. Luke tells us more than once was pondering these things in her heart, did meditate much on the question. Yet she knew too how to accept with magnificent faith that which human minds can understand but imperfectly at best.

St. Paul was later to write some remarkable lines about the nothingness of all creatures. To the Philippians he said: [5] "It is God who works in you both the will and the accomplishment." In other words, when you do anything good, recognize that not only the external performance of good, "the accomplishment", but even the interior good decision of the will is God's work, not yours. He expressed it forcefully to the Corinthians: [6] "What have you that you have not received? But if you have received" it from God "why brag as if you had not received" it from Him, but instead, had produced the good yourself? St. Augustine wrote of this truth with remarkable vehemence: [7] "When God crowns our merits, He crowns His own gifts." Some have thought Augustine exaggerated. But if we realize what St. Paul was saying, that he really did mean that there is no good that we are or have or do that we do not receive from God, then we are forced to confess that our very merits are God's gifts.

Should we, as it were, move back deeper into the process of doing good, and say: "At least, I got the good idea of doing the good"? But no, St. Paul again confronts us with: [8] "We are not sufficient to think anything by ourselves as from ourselves, but our sufficiency is from God." And of course, if we have no good that we have not received: how could we claim even the good thought? [9]

If we see, then, and deeply realize that no good comes from us, we are reduced to a state of nothingness. And when we add that we not only cannot claim credit for good, but yet do deserve blame for the evil we do, then indeed our self-esteem literally falls below the zero line.

Mary, of course, had no sin, she did not therefore have to charge herself with falling below zero. But not even she, with a "dignity second only to God" could claim to have produced by herself the least good.

What then of the fact that the Church, guided by the Holy Spirit, praise her virtue, extols her dignity? What of the fact that inspired Scripture itself tells us that we are sharers [10] in the divine nature by grace? What of the confident words of St. Paul awaiting execution: [11] "As for the rest, there is ready for me the crown of righteousness, which the Lord, the just Judge, will give me on that day, not only to me, but to all who have loved His coming"?

We need to realize that there are as it were two levels on which we can speak of ourselves, the fundamental or rock-bottom level, and the secondary level. On the fundamental level, we must speak as we have done, must confess that we have nothing that we have not received. Yet, on the secondary level, what we have received is really ours, what He gives us belongs to us. He will reward us for what we do, on the secondary level, with the crown of righteousness. This is really due us, from the "just Judge". We are, then, both wonderful and nothing. How, we cannot fully realize on this side of the great veil. But we can hold both truths, in the darkness of faith. Mary held to both with all her heart. She was glad not to have recognition. She knew that on the second level, she deserved it, and foretold that all generations would call her blessed. On the fundamental level, she knew that she had nothing she had not received, and was pleased at not being recognized.

Her realization of her total dependence on God was most deep, penetrating to the depths of her being. Some persons who seem religious will say to themselves, and to others: "I have done much for God. But I admit that I am nothing. I am the least of His servants." Such a statement *can* involve a most dangerous self-deception. The Pharisee who scorned the Publican in the Temple began his prayer by saying: [12] "O God, I give thanks to you that I am not like the rest of men ... " He admitted he was doing more than others, and he seemed to attribute it all to God: "I give thanks *to you*". Yet we know the judgment of the Divine Master who searches hearts: his prayer was rejected as hypocritical, in spite of words that seemed to give all credit to God. He was, we gather, deceiving himself, telling himself he admitted he was good, but that that was quite all right, as long as he attributed everything to God.

Now of course, that would have been all right, if only he had, in the depths of his being, really known, deeply realized his nothingness. With such realization, a saint, such as St. Paul, could even tell his converts: [13] "Be imitators of me, as I am of Christ." Mary too had such a depth of humility, for humility is not self-deception, but the virtue that makes us deeply know and fully embrace the truth about ourselves: that we are nothing, that all the good we are, have and do is from God.

She loved humility and non-recognition too because she knew, even before her Son preached it, how much God hates pride: [14] "He resists the proud, but gives grace to the lowly." Christ showed the greatest mercy to sinners, to all but one kind of sinners. He had no patience with the pride of the Pharisees. Them He called [15] "whitewashed tombs. Outwardly you seem beautiful, but inside you are full of dead men's bones and all uncleanness." Humility is not the greatest of the virtues. That is love. But it is a peculiarly *fundamental* virtue: St. Augustine [16] compares it to the foundation of a building. The taller the building, the deeper must the foundation be. How deep must have been the foundation of humility in her whose dignity was to be "second only to God"!

Furthermore, the Jewish theologians of her time [17] insisted on the same truth which we saw in chapter 10, that there is a moral order, with which God is concerned. He wishes it to be balanced. Hence sin is considered as a *debt*. When someone sins, the scales must be balanced. Now Mary knew, and felt deeply, the deficiency in the reverence given to God. Of course, she did not have to listen to men taking the name of God in vain, as we do today. For several centuries before her day, the Jews had become so impressed with the sanctity of the name "Yahweh" that even in reading the Scriptures, they would never pronounce it. Only the High Priest could say that word, and he did it just once a year, in reading inspired Scripture in the solemn liturgy of the Day of Atonement. But she knew that in myriad other ways—by all manner of sins—honour was being denied Him. To balance that defect in the scales of righteousness, she gladly acquiesced in her own non-recognition.

But she knew too that a lowly status was very beneficial to her personally. Acceptance of the will of God for us includes everything, even a lack of recognition, even positive disdain and unfair treatment from others. It is far easier for us to see the will of God in such things as sickness, misfortunes caused by *inanimate* nature. But when trials come through the wickedness of another *human* being, then the level of difficulty is sharply raised. Our pride is not hurt when inanimate things cause us pain; but it is galling to be slighted by a being who should know better. Further, we see inescapably, that this person here and now is acting *contrary to the will of God*. We quite properly react against that. To see even some aspect of it as the will of God for us is specially difficult precisely because of the fact that we see the act as basically *against* the will of God. Yet as we indicated, there is an aspect in which this is the will of God for us. He does not will that anyone should do what is wrong to us, but He does will that we accept it as due to our sins. It is true, we perhaps do not deserve *this particular thing* at *this time* from *this person*. But by our sins, we do deserve the equivalent, and more besides. So we need to say to ourselves: "Perhaps this slight or offense is unfair, unjust here and now. But I am accepting it as the just recompense for things in which I did not receive the penalty that really was due to me." And, even wihout thinking of the fact that such things are richly due to our sins, we can look at the positive side, and say that even though someone else is acting wrongly, for us to accept it by way of atonement, to help balance the moral order, [18] is something that pleases God, something He wills.

Of course, Mary could never say any slight or mistreatment was owed to her sins, for she was sinless. But she could, and did, gladly accept such things for the sake of atonement for the sins of others.

Furthermore, she knew there was a different kind of advantage for her personally. She could see, what we all see, that all too often those who receive recognition become proud. And those who gain actual power, are not infrequently corrupted by it. The flattery that commonly surrounds a man in a position of authority tends to damage his judgment. He is constantly being told what his subjects think he will like to hear. They never speak of his faults, never blame him. We are all in danger of excessive opinions of ourselves. When others provide no corrective against that, but instead, praise a man: that man is in much danger of believing he really is wonderful, and he can become even, in some cases, a monster of pride and arrogance. A lowly position protects one from such dangers.

Still more importantly, Mary knew well what St. Paul proclaimed so often and so forcefully: she knew that a man is made holy to the precise degree that he is not just a member of Christ, but is like Christ. She knew her Son [19] "emptied Himself, taking on the form of a slave, being made in the likeness of man ... He lowered Himself, being made obedient even to death, death on a cross." She rejoiced to be like Him. She knew well what Vatican II was to teach that the practice of poverty, chastity, and obedience [20] "continually arouses the fervour of love, and especially [is] able to make the Christian person more and more conformed to the virginal way of life in poverty which Christ the Lord chose for Himself, and which His Virgin Mother embraced."

NOTES

1. On the Church § 56.
2. **Ibid.** § 56.
3. Cf. Chap. 8 above.

4. Pius XI, **Lux veritatis,** Dec. 25, 1931: AAS 23,513.

5. Phil. 2,13.

6. 1 Cor. 4,7.

7. Epistle 164,5,19: **Patrologia Latina** 33,880.

8. 2 Cor. 3,5. Cf. Second Council of Orange, Canons 4-7 on grace, in Denzinger-Schönmetzer, **Enchiridion Symbolorum** 374-77 (DB 177-180). Because of special papal approval these canons of a local council amount to solemn definitions.

9. Cf. W. Most, **New Answers to Old Questions** (St. Paul Publications, London, 1971) Chap. 7.

10. Cf. 2 Pet. 1,4.

11. 2 Tim. 4,8.

12. Lk. 18,11.

13. 1 Cor. 11,1.

14. 1 Pet. 5,5.

15. Mt. 23,27.

16. **Sermo** 69,1,2.

17. Cf. S. Lyonnet and L. Sabourin, **Sin, Redemption and Sacrifice,** (Pontifical Biblical Institute, Rome, 1970) 32-33.

18. Cf. Chap. 10 above.

19. Phil. 2,7-8.

20. On the Church § 46.

16 — PONDERING IN OUR HEARTS WITH MARY

Vatican II, in describing the reaction of Mary after finding her Son in the Temple, echoes the words of the Gospel: [1] "In a meditative way, she kept all these words of His in her heart." In the same document, the Council warns priests that their apostolic work should not crush the spirit of meditation, but instead, should be fed by it: [2] "... realizing what they do and imitating what they handle [in the Mass] instead of being crushed by the cares, dangers and burdens of the apostolate, let them rather ascend through them to higher sanctity by nourishing and warming their activities through an abundance of meditation, to the delight of the whole Church of God." Religious too are urged [3] "to learn the 'eminent knowledge of Jesus Christ' by reading the divine Scriptures and meditation."

To imitate Mary's pondering in her heart is good not only for priests and religious, but for all. For it consists simply in uniting our minds and our wills with God, by thinking on divine truths, and then stirring up our wills to align better with His will.

Before taking up the practical means of carrying out meditation, we might focus on one special aspect of it, namely, the role of our minds in meditation. There are two ways of knowing something, notional knowledge, and realized knowledge. Suppose I read in the news that there is a famine somewhere in Asia. I will probably believe the news report, but yet I may not be specially influenced by it: after all, such reports are all too frequent. This is notional knowledge. But suppose I were to go to the famine area, see people actually suffering, perhaps even dying of starvation. I would then know of it, but in a different way. Then my knowledge would be *realized*, and it would surely drive me to act.

There are, obviously, many degrees on this scale in which knowledge can pass from a mere notional knowledge, to a deeply realized knowledge. It is evident that if my faith is to be vivid, I will need to try to bring my knowledge as far as possible along that scale towards fullest realization. For realization is dynamic. Someone has aptly said that then we not merely live *with* faith, we live *by* faith, that is, faith becomes dynamic, a driving force, not just something that we carry about in a sort of inert condition. For if we realized the truths of faith as vividly as we do today's major sports event, then for sure, we would be much different.

We saw in chapter 10 that we dispose ourselves for a deeper and stronger faith by acting on faith, by living our lives in the way a man does who deeply believes in, and almost sees with his eyes the spiritual realities. We need to add that faith is deepened not only by action, but also by meditation on the truths of faith.

Is a general spirit of reflection or recollection or frequent realization of the presence of God sufficient for this purpose? Such a general spirit is of course a help. But we really need to take time out to accomplish much. As little as fifteen minutes a day would make a great difference in the spiritual growth of anyone who cares to make the investment.

How go about meditation? Many very elaborate methods have been proposed. Today, it is the fashion to ridicule or at least disregard them. But really, we would do better if we were to confess that people are very different, each from the other. And further, there are tides and trends that vary from age to age. These elaborate procedures probably were quite helpful in other times. In fact, it is likely that some persons today—for people are all different—would find them beneficial. But for most persons today, a more informal approach seems to be preferable.

We might begin by just taking time out, as it were, for a moment, to let our mental engines stop racing. We could try to recall and to begin to realize what we know is true, that God is present everywhere. We may prefer to think of Him as pervading even the vastness of interstellar or intergalactic space; or we may find it better to think of the special presence He has in our souls by grace.

After this toning-up exercise, we begin the actual meditation, unless, of course, we find such thoughts as suggested engage our attention so that we want to dwell on them. Then there is no need to move on to anything else. And that will happen to not a few persons on various occasions.

There are several ways of starting. Probably most persons will find the soak-in approach very good. Most of us will need some good book to help us, a book that presents well the basic truths of faith. We read far enough in the book to find a spot which strikes us as worth dwelling on. Then we put down the book for a while and as it were hold that thought before the eyes of our mind, with the idea of trying to *realize* it, to let it soak into our consciousness. In the course of doing this we may feel the need of divine help, and informally ask for that. Or we may find ourselves inclined to make some prayerful comment. Suppose for instance, we were reading something on the greatness of the majesty of God. Perhaps it was just the psalm line: [4] "O Lord, our Lord, how great is your name throughout all the earth." We could hold before our mind's eye the thought of His infinity, and contrast it with our nothingness. We interiorly feel like bowing to the dust, expressing the fact that we are nothing compared to Him. The writer of this

Psalm felt that reaction: [5] "What is man, that you remember him? or the son of man, that you visit him?"

We may be able to hold that thought, that attitude for perhaps thirty seconds. Then it begins to fade into vagueness or mere reverie. At that point we may be able, by rereading the line in our book, to bring it back again and reuse it, just as before. Perhaps the same cycle may repeat a few more times. But then we will find the need to move on in our book to find another passage that will help us.

Some, instead of allowing some simple thought to soak in, do better if they develop an idea, from step to step. For example, they might take that same thought of the immensity of God and expand it, by using some data from astronomy: I look to the northern sky and see, if I know just where to look and have a small telescope, the galaxy of Andromeda. It is really comparable to a universe all by itself. It is the closest of the "island universes" to our own. How far? So distant that astronomers estimate it takes light between one and one-half and two million years to reach us, racing at the speed of something over 186,000 miles per second. Yet God made that, not with careful planning and immense labour, but by simply saying: Let it be. And He loves me, and pays attention to me!

Others, though they are less numerous, will be able to take a Gospel incident and as it were give it a replay in their mind, just as if a movie or TV film were repeating it for them. Some can even think of themselves as present, and converse with some of the persons who take part in that episode.

We already noticed that we may find ourselves inclined to add some spontaneous, informal prayer, perhaps even of a conversational character, while we are thinking or contemplating. Whether we do that in the course of our con-

125

siderations, or after, is not important. But it is important to try to get it in somewhere. Really, it is almost natural to want to talk over, with God Himself, or with Mary, some of the things we have been thinking about. If we *realize* the basic truths they should stimulate us to want to do something. Perhaps I may discuss what improvement in policy is suitable *for me*, at this *present time*. Or we may notice how far short we fall of what we should be, in relation to the truths of faith. And for sure, we should see that we need, in any words, formal or informal, to ask for divine help to improve.

It is important, as we said, to have both of the elements that we have discussed, namely, thoughts and informal conversations. Really, this means that we are uniting both mind and will to God. We unite our minds, by thinking about His truths, by trying to realize them. We should also unite our wills, by talking with Him, by laying plans to better align our wills with His will.

The proportion of these two elements, the work of the mind, and the work of the will, is apt to be very lopsided when we first take up meditation, and probably for a long period thereafter: the work of the mind takes up most of the time we devote to meditation. But over a period of time—the length of the period varies much in individual cases, but it is not apt to be short—there is likely to be a shift in proportion, so that we spend more time on the phase in which our wills are active.

After that second stage, though some may be led by grace to omit that second stage, there comes a third stage of the development of meditation in which we find that we can use the "soak-in" technique described above, but we will be able to have many more cycles from the one thought with its matching attitude; we can spend even an entire fifteen minutes or more without the need of going on to other considerations. Some call this stage the prayer of simplicity. The reason for the name is obvious: there is need of only one thought, and one response to it.

We mentioned that general habitual recollection is not enough, that we need to spend a longer time on meditation. But the fact that we do give ourselves a certain period for meditation daily not only should not dispense from efforts at recollection and frequent if not constant awareness of the presence of God; but habitual recollection in turn tends to deepen meditation. In a later chapter [6] we will return to this matter of habitual recollection, and suggest some means of cultivating it.

As we said before, we probably will use a book to help us during the time of meditation. It is helpful to look over the book the day before, to find spots that will be most helpful to us. Further, spiritual reading in general, including reading other than directly meditative matter, helps make us more apt for meditation.

St. Alphonsus [7] long ago made a very apt comment on meditation. He said that whereas a man might be able to continue with many other religious exercises without giving up a sinful way of life, the case is different with meditation: he will either give up meditation, or give up his sinful ways. For meditation, pondering in our hearts in imitation of Mary, is dynamic. We cannot *realize* divine truths, and remain unmoved. That is why she never tired of pondering in her heart the words and deeds of her divine Son.

NOTES

.. On the Church § 57. Cf. Lk. 2, 51.

2. On the Church § 41.

3. On Religious Life § 6, citing Phil. 3,8.

4. Ps. 8,1.

5. Ps. 8,5.

6. In Chap. 18.

7. **Praxis Confessarii,** n. 122.

17 — MYSTICAL ROSE

If by imitating Mary's pondering in her heart, we advance in meditation, we will be likely to find that after some time, our meditation will tend to simplify. How soon this will take place will vary in individual cases, and according to several factors. Most prominent among them will be our mortification, the alignment of our wills with the will of God, our love of lowliness, and our habitual recollection.

In this simpler form of meditation, as we described it in the last chapter, we find that we can hold just a single simple thought before our minds, realizing it ever more deeply, and responding in our wills by an attitude appropriate to the thought, e.g., an attitude of adoration. When the soul reaches this stage, this process, in cycles as it were, can be repeated, using just the one thought, for fifteen to thirty minutes.

But there are far reaching realms of development possible even beyond this point. Some souls reach what is called infused contemplation. And there are many stages and degrees within it too. It is not only not wrong, it is good for anyone who is in earnest about pleasing God as fully as possible, to desire to reach this infused contemplation. Actually though it is found in only a minority of souls, yet it is more frequent than is commonly supposed. Some have it without knowing what is happening. For this reason, the help of a director, who is both learned in theology, and experienced in these matters, is very important. Many theologians think it is impossible for any soul to reach full maturity, spiritual perfection, without experiencing infused contemplation. Such seems to be the view of St. John of the Cross [1] and St. Teresa of Avila, Doctors of the Church, who knew it well both theologically and from personal experience.

St. John of the Cross seems to say it will definitely occur at the end of the first major phase of the spiritual life, which is called the Purgative Way. In the Purgative Way, a man does what he can to rid himself of his faults, even mere imperfections. The work cannot be completed without a special action of the Holy Spirit. That of course, is always given if one makes himself not indisposed to it. [2] The appearance of infused contemplation in well defined form marks the border, the transition from this Purgative Way into the Illuminative Way, with its higher forms of contemplation. That Illuminative Way ends in a severe trial, which St. John calls the Dark Night of the Soul. Beyond it lies the still more marvelous realm called the Unitive Way, in which is found the greatest possible perfection to which a soul can attain in this life. Mary surely must have attained that. For, as we have already seen, Pope Pius IX said that her holiness or spiritual perfection even at the start was so great that "none greater under God can be thought of, and no one but God can comprehend it."

But to return to our attempt to picture the development of meditation. When one has reached the simple form of meditation described earlier, and has continued in it for some time, a further simplification normally takes place. When one began this simple form of meditation, he could use a great variety of thoughts for it. But with further progress, he will find that the only thought will seem to be the Divinity itself, without any mental image. Within this stage, there will sometimes come as it were rays of infused light: one suddenly "sees" divine truth as never before, and has a remarkably new kind of awareness of God. It is a sort of simple, loving gaze at Him. It is not produced by human activity, but by the special action of the Holy Spirit. The soul itself is basically passive, as it were, doing no more than holding its eyes open.

Such flashes may come at any time, not only during a regular meditation period. In fact, in some souls, they are more apt to come at the most unexpected and unpredictable moments, perhaps when one is walking down the stairs, or even when he is busy with something else.

Oftentimes there is a warmth of love that is felt, but it is totally different from the feelings or consolations described in chapter 14. These mere consolations are as it were on the surface; the warmth of this light of the Spirit wells up [3] from within the depths of the soul, and from there overflows, sometimes, into the realm of mere feeling. There is nothing else in human experience like it. As a result, if one has never had such an experience, it is impossible to convey a clear impression of it. It is similar to the problem of giving a colour blind person a good mental image of a rainbow: since it is based on things entirely outside his experience, he cannot really picture it, even though one may give him the figures for the wave lengths of the various colours.

Sometimes there is no warmth, nothing like a feeling at all; the soul may be in a state of spiritual dryness.

These bits of light at first are very brief, may come at any time, and are not always necessarily restricted to just the simple perfection of the Divinity itself: they may result instead in a hitherto unknown (to that person) depth of realization of other spiritual things, e.g., the nothingness of creatures. But when there is further progress, the soul will perceive only the Divinity itself, without any image, in a vague sort of way, with the impression of a contact with God as real and concrete as one has when, for example, he puts his hand on a table.

When such an experience is well developed, there is usually a sort of instinct that tells one not even to move, for fear that would disturb or drive away the special experience. In fact, one feels that even to use any words for prayer, even mentally, would be out of place. Later, of course, regular prayer is in place, is called for. But not at that instant. The loving gaze itself is a lofty form of prayer.

Obviously, there is much room for self-deception or auto-suggestion here. To avoid that, one needs much to have a learned and experienced director, if he is to be had.

St. John of the Cross gives some signs [4] to help determine whether a soul has really reached this infused contemplation. First, there is a great aridity: the soul finds no pleasure in creatures. But neither does it have any consolation from divine things: all is barren. As a result, although formerly the person may have found it not too difficult to make sacrifices, to practice mortification, now these things are *more* difficult. Yet, in spite of this arid state, there is a persistent awareness of God. Distractions of course come, but the awareness comes back persistently, of its own accord (actually, it is the work of the Holy Spirit) after the distraction. This consciousness of God is indistinct and obscure, without any image. Yet it is very real. Along with this awareness goes a greater desire, though without pleasure, to serve Him well. In this, of course, the soul is growing, growing in the darkness of faith. [5] Added to these two signs is an inability to practice meditation in the step-by-step process described in chapter 16. Of course, many souls never do find that step-by-step procedure very well adapted to them. So this third sign is less useful.

It is necessary to find *all* of these signs before we can have any confidence in thinking we are dealing with a well-developed case of infused contemplation. For an aridity can come from attachment to creatures, from sin. But when an aridity is coupled with the second sign we have mentioned, then we know it must have a different source.

We have mentioned that in infused contemplation there is no image of God in the mind of the recipient. Not only is no image called for, but any image would be a hindrance. Souls at this point find even the thought of the Humanity of Christ an obstacle. [6] Now that Sacred Humanity is the very instrument of our salvation, and surely is not in itself an obstacle. Rather, this phenomenon comes from the fact that the soul is in a transitional stage. It is still too weak, as it were, to hold simultaneously to the newly found contemplation and still be able to think of the Humanity of Christ. Later, when it has gone farther, that problem will disappear. The case is similar with the thought of Mary.

But we should add that although to think of Mary in a physical way would be a hindrance, there is another way in which the soul may be aware of her. Some cases [7] have been reported of an infused contemplation in which the presence of Mary is perceived, as united to the Divinity. After all, she is more closely united with God than any other creature. So, when the Divinity itself becomes the object of contemplation, there is no inherent reason why she, so united to Him, could not be also part of that object. In such a case, of course, she is perceived without any image, with no thought of her bodily nature, even though that has been glorified by the Assumption. One simply finds her included in the vague but intensely real object of the loving gaze. Of course, not all souls that reach infused contemplation also have this special contemplation of Mary, not even all those who are specially devout to her. When and if that is to be granted is the prerogative of the Holy Spirit to decide.

Beyond the first experience of infused contemplation lie many higher forms, as we have said. A soul that has reached the point we described has absolutely no reason to consider itself a Saint. St. John of the Cross says that such a person is still only at the outer edge of the lowest of the three Ways, the Purgative Way. To reach full perfection, there is still a long road to travel. Part of it may be in the pleasures of the warm form of contemplation, but much of it is certain to be enmeshed in trials, terrible trials and temptations. At least the soul now knows to a slight degree what God is, for it has received a dim glimpse, as if the veil between this world and the next were opened just a little. Can it still fall back into sin and go backward spiritually? Sadly, the answer is yes. It must count much on the help of Mary, to avoid that, and to advance ever further until the endless day dawns, when there will be not just the vague dim awareness of contact, but brilliant, face to face vision.

NOTES

1. Cf. St. John of the Cross, **Dark Night** 1,8,1.

2. Cf. St. John of the Cross, **Living Flame of Love** 3,46-47: "If in this way the soul is free of all these things, which is . . . that which the soul is able to accomplish, it is impossible, when it does its part, that God should fail to do that which is His part in communicating Himself, at least in secret and in silence. It is more impossible than that the sun should fail to shine in a clear and open sky; for just as the sun rises in the morning to enter your house if the shutters are opened, thus God... will enter into the soul that is empty and fill it with divine goods."

3. Cf. St. Teresa of Avila, **Interior Castle** 4,2.

4. St. John of the Cross, **Dark Night**, 1,9, and **Ascent of Mt. Carmel** 2,13. These three signs need

not yet be present for some preliminary flashes of light from the Gifts.

5. Cf. Chap. 8 above.

6. The thought of the Sacred Humanity of Christ is of course good in itself. The inability to combine it with this state comes from the weakness of the soul at first, in getting accustomed to contemplation. Later, it will be able to return to that thought. Cf. St. Teresa of Avila, **Interior Castle** 6,7.

7. Cf. V. Hoppenbrouwers, O. Carm., "The Blessed Mother Teaches Us to Pray" in: **Analecta Ordinis Carmelitarum** XVI (1951) II, 259-65; L. Reypens, "Marie et la Mystique" in Du Manoir, **Maria** (Beauchesne, Paris, 1949) I,760-63; Ven. Michael of St. Augustine, "The Mariform and Marian Life in Mary, for Mary", in "McGinnis (ed.) **Life with Mary**.

18 — CONSECRATION TO MARY

The highest, most complete form of Marian devotion lies in making and living out a total consecration to her.

As we saw in chapter 6, Pope Paul VI actually renewed a consecration of the whole world to the Immaculate Heart of Mary, on the very floor of the Council, at the solemn close of the third session, on November 21, 1964. In doing so, he explicitly recalled the previous consecration made by Pope Pius XII. On May 13, 1967, on the occasion of his own unprecedented visit to the great Marian shrine of Fatima, Pope Paul issued an Apostolic Exhortation, in which he spoke of this event of November 21, 1964, and added: [1] "We urge all the sons of the Church that they individually consecrate themselves again to the Immaculate Heart of the Mother of the Church, and, by carrying over this outstanding sign of devotion into the living of their lives, become more and more conformed to the divine will, and that by devoutly imitating the examples of their heavenly Queen, they serve her as sons."

As we saw in chapter 6, Vatican II gave us a brilliant theological foundation for the fullest possible form of living out of a consecration to Mary. It did this by showing that the Father has freely willed to give her an all-pervading place in all His dealings with us. As a result, we noticed, it is most logical that we give her a similarly all-pervading place in our response to Him.

Of course, there are great variations from one individual to another in the spiritual life. From the fact that any given thing is *objectively* the best, it does not follow that this particular individual should take it up. Rather, Divine Providence adapts itself to the differences of individuals, and gives varied graces to various persons. As a result, not all are moved to follow the fullest form of Marian consecration. It is most important to keep that fact constantly in mind in reading this chapter. For we are going to present the maximum in Marian consecration. Not everyone should follow everything: let each, following the varieties of grace with supernatural prudence, decide whether to follow all or part and which parts of what we will say.

There are two phases to a complete consecration, the making of the consecration itself, and the living out of that consecration.

We can get a helpful lead on the fullest meaning of the first of these phases from the words of Pope Leo XIII on consecration to the Sacred Heart of Jesus: [2] "For we, in dedicating ourselves, not only recognize and accept His rule explicitly and freely, but we actually bear witness that if that which we give were ours, we would most willingly give it. And we ask Him to graciously accept from us that very thing, even though it is already His."

Pope Leo tells us that consecration involves acceptance of the dominion which Christ already has over us, in such a way that we acknowledge that anything we could give Him is really already His. But we ask Him to kindly accept it none the less, as though we were not bound to it already. The reason is simple: Christ as King of the Universe, by that very fact alone has most absolute rights to our service. There is nothing we could possibly do that He could not demand, even with no promise of reward. Yet the fact is that He, in His generosity, does want us to present our service to Him as if we did not already owe it to Him.

Now Vatican II has told us that in the Assumption,

135

Mary [3] "was taken up, body and soul, to heavenly glory, and was exalted as Queen of the universe by the Lord." On the same subject, Pius XII had written earlier: [4] "And her domain is as vast as that of her Son and God, for nothing is exempt from her dominion." We should not think of her dominion as something as it were separate from that of her Son: no, in royal rule as in all else, she forms a sort of unitary principle with Him. Just as her offering melted together with His on Calvary, so as to form the one great price of Redemption, so her Queenship and His Kingship are one authority, inseparable.

We can easily see then, that we can, with theological exactness, say much the same of consecration to her as Pope Leo XIII said of consecration to Christ the King. We recognize by our consecration that she, as Queen of the Universe with Him, already has fullest rights to our service. We gladly accept that fact, and ask her to graciously accept our offering, to which she already has a right, as if it were not due her by the very fact of her Queenship.

St. Louis de Montfort, in his outstanding book, *True Devotion*, points out that a complete consecration involves giving to Mary the right to dispose of all the spiritual goods which we can validly and licitly give into her hands. That means that we give her the right to the final word on what our prayers, mortifications, satisfactions are to be used for. We may, in this framework, often pray for specific intentions. Really, she wants us to pray most earnestly for the needs of the Church, our country, our parents and dear ones and all towards whom we have obligations. She will actually take better care of them than we could, for her power as Queen is such that [5] "nothing is exempt from her dominion", and her love for them is even greater than ours is. [6] But yet, in acknowledgment of her Queenly dominion, we gladly give her the final say. Of course, some things, e.g.

136

personal spiritual growth [7] are such that by their very nature they cannot be given to anyone else. That is understood in this arrangement.

We heartily agree with this plea of St. Louis de Montfort: it is evident that no consecration could be called complete without including these features. We would merely add this comment: some souls have been overly preoccupied with this aspect of consecration, so much so that they tend to overlook other, even more important aspects of consecration, those namely, that we will shortly explain.

We could add to this something we already proposed in chapter 11, namely, that we give to her as it were a "Power of Attorney". That is, we appoint her to speak for us to the Father, so that she can make in our name, any offer to accept any specific future trials which it might please Him to have us make. In this way we more actively align our wills with the will of the Father, and we do it in a way that imitates most closely His own ways. For He has freely decreed, as we said, to give her an all-pervading role in all His dealings with us: by this arrangement we try to give her a similarly all-pervading place in our response to Him.

Once we have made our consecration, with or without some solemnity, the important thing is to live it out. We could sum up the chief features of that under three headings.

First, we live in the consciousness of our dependence on her. She is our Queen, our spiritual Mother, the one on whom, next to her Son, we depend for everything. All grace comes to us through her hands. She has the right, for we have given it to her, to dispose of all our spiritual goods insofar as they are disposable. She has even the right, as our "Attorney" to make offers in our name to the Father.

In a sense, we pray only through her. This does not mean that we never address our prayers to the Father, to her Son, or to other Saints. Very definitely we should continue to do so at certain times, while at other times we address them directly to her. The practical details and proportions of this are to be worked out in individual instances, with the help of the light of graces she will obtain for us. But even when we speak directly to the Father or to the Son, or to the Divine Spirit, we try to be aware at least in a general way that we depend on her merits and intercession for everything. For she shared with her Son in earning all graces. As a result, whatever is given us, is given through the merits and satisfactions of Jesus and Mary, operating, as we said, as a unit, as one.

Secondly, it is good to try to live in her presence. For there is a real sense in which she is always present to us. Loosely, she can be said to be present by her love, for when there is a mutual love between two, that love constitutes a sort of presence. But more importantly, since her Assumption, though she still has a body, yet it is a glorified body, and, more importantly, she now operates in the way in which a spirit does. [8] We say a spirit is present wherever it makes its effects felt, for spirits do not have the same sort of relation to space that we have. Spirits need no space at all. And we recall the way the risen body of her Son seemed to ignore space and time, passing through doors without any need to open them, becoming visible when He wished, not visible when He did not wish. It is much the same with her. But the chief point is this: She is always having her effect on us inasmuch as every grace we receive comes to us through her. [9]

All souls benefit much by learning to live in the frequent, almost constant, in some cases, awareness of the presence of God. A soul specially dedicated to Mary, realizing her close union with the Divinity, rightly tries to cultivate the awareness of her along with that of God.

How do this? Different souls will prefer different means

of cultivating this awareness. Some employ conditioned reflexes, e.g., they form the habit of saying some ejaculation or other brief prayer every time they enter their room, or go up or down steps, or do some other familiar thing. At first, a special effort is needed; in time, one almost automatically begins to say such a prayer in such circumstances. The prayer is valuable both in itself, and as a means of recalling her presence. Others like the method of "small talk". That is, as they go about their regular occupations, they often speak informally to Mary, merely telling her what they are doing, how it is going, asking for light, for help. This is not the most exalted prayer, but it is a good prayer, a helpful means of contact.

This awareness of her presence of course cannot really be constant. It must be interrupted. We work for an explicit fully conscious awareness at some times, and are content with, at most, a vague background consciousness at other times. [10]

Thirdly, we can cultivate an increasing realization of the fact that since she shares in the royal dominion of Christ the King, when we obey Him, we are at the same time obeying her. We gladly accept this fact.

What does she want us to do? Obviously, she wants us to obey all legitimate commands of all lawful authorities; she wants us to make the best use of providentially sent mortifications, so that we not only do not complain, but actually welcome them with joy. [11] But, when we have done all these things, there remain many other decisions to be made, both large and small, in the practical management of our daily lives. How can we know her will in these matters? There is no certain and easy way to determine the answer. Of course, we should try to imitate her, especially in the ways suggested in previous chapters. But also, when we must make a decision, we do well to begin by asking her to obtain light for us. Then, in her presence, we try *to think out*—being careful not to let vague feelings that strike us seem to be divine inspirations—what she would do. We do not try to project present situations back into first century Nazareth. Rather, we consider what she would do in present circumstances. A special safeguard against illusions lies in consulting a good spiritual director. That does not absolve us of all responsibility. To attempt to escape responsibility in such a way would be contrary to spiritual growth. But we need the help of another, especially for the sake of objectivity. No one can be completely objective about his own affairs, especially when there is question of parting with some creature or pleasure. We tend to go to extremes in such matters. Most of us go to the easy extreme, but human nature has enough of the pendulum characteristic in it to make us quite capable of reacting to the opposite extreme as well. Another person, simply because he is another person, can help much. Most of all, a director should be well versed in ascetic and mystical theology. He should also be a very spiritual man himself. Not always can we obtain such help. But when we can, it would be folly not to make use of it.

Further, it is universal experience that the mere process of trying to explain ourselves to someone else helps clarify our own mind.

If then, each according to the type of graces given him, tries by such means to bring Mary into every facet of his spiritual life, he will be most closely imitating the ways of the Father, who, as we have repeatedly said, chose to employ her at every point of His dealings with us.

NOTES

1. Paul VI, **Signum magnum:** AAS 59,475.

2. Leo XIII, **Annum sacrum,** May 25, 1899: ASS 31,646.

3. On the Church § 59.

4. Pius XII, **Bendito seia,** May 13, 1946: AAS 38,266.

5. Cf. n. 4 above.

6. Cf. Chap. 12 above.

7. Condign merit is by nature inalienable.

8. Cf. 1 Cor. 15,44.

9. Cf. note 10 on Chap. 4 above.

10. This is related to the question of Marian contemplation: cf. note 7 on Chap. 17 above.

11. Cf. Chap. 11 above.

19 — MASS WITH MARY

Pope John XXIII made a very remarkable statement in a Radio message to the 16th Eucharistic Congress of Italy, on September 13, 1959. It seems to contain a wonderful theological implication which, strangely, has attracted no notice. After expressing the hope that all the people of Italy would be strengthened in their fervour and veneration for the Blessed Virgin, "the Mother of the Mystical Body, of which the Eucharist is the symbol and vital center," he continued: [1] "We trust that they will imitate in her the most perfect model of union with Jesus, our Head; we trust that they will join Mary in the offering of the Divine Victim . . ."

We naturally ask ourselves: To what offering of the Divine Victim is the Pope referring? Of course, he at least presupposes her union with him in the great sacrifice of Calvary. [2] But we wonder if there is not something more. For the Pope was speaking to a Eucharistic Congress, and he referred to Mary, as we saw as "the Mother of the Mystical Body of which the Eucharist is the symbol and vital center." So it would, to say the least, not be straining his words to suppose he referred to her joining with her Son in the renewal of Calvary, the Eucharistic sacrifice.

Vatican II, in its constitution on the Divine Liturgy, [3] called the Mass the renewal of the New Covenant. Centuries before, the Council of Trent had taught the same thing, observing also that [4] "only the mode of offering is different" between the Mass and Calvary, that is, the original was

142

bloody, while the renewal is unbloody. Now if that be the only difference between the original and the renewal, then Mary should be united with the renewal too, just as she was in the original sacrifice. [5] And that is likely to be what Pope John referred to when he urged the people of Italy to "join Mary in the offering of the Divine Victim." After all, he could not suggest joining with her in the *past* offering, the one she made on Calvary. So, he ought to mean the only offering in which they could join, the ever-present renewal of Calvary in the Mass. [6]

How could this be? We recall that there are two aspects to a sacrifice, that is, the external sign, and the interior dispositions which that outer sign expresses.

Mary has a very obvious union with both aspects of the Mass. First, the outward sign is the renewal of the death of her Son. But she is the one from whom He received the very flesh and blood that become present on our altars.

She is also united with the interior dispositions of her Son. Just as He, in the glory of Heaven, still renews the the offering of His obedience, [7] His willingness to die again, were the Father to ask that, so too she has not changed the dispositions of her heart. She once consented to His offering, at tremendous cost to herself. She has not withdrawn that consent. Her will is now not less aligned with the will of the Father and the will of her Son than when she was still upon this earth.

So, quite obviously, she still is most closely united with the Mass, both in its interior and in its exterior aspects. Rightly then could Pope John urge the people of Italy to join with her in the offering she makes in the Eucharist.

In a very real sense, it is impossible not to be united with Mary in the Mass. For if two persons are each most closely joined to a third, then, whether they realize it or not, they are joined to each other. So, if we are closely joined with Christ at Mass, and she too, obviously, is closely joined with Him: then the more closely we are joined with Him, the more closely we are joined with her too.

Of course, we should not be content with this as it were automatic union with her. As Pope John urges, we should consciously and deliberately capitalize on this union, and be gladly aware of our special closeness to her in the Mass.

Again, as we saw in chapter 3, all the members of Christ are called upon to join their obedient dispositions with His in the renewal of Calvary. We saw that this twofold offering, melting into one, is parallel to the twofold offering that took place in the original sacrifice, in which Mary was joined with Christ so closely that her offering fused with His into the one great price of Redemption. We now can add: the two-fold offering of the Mass includes that of Christ the Head, that of Mary, and that of the ordinary members of Christ.

St. Augustine made a specially rich comment on the Mass. In it, he said, [8] "the Church, since it is the body of this Head, learns through Him to offer herself." Christ became obedient even to the point of death, even to death on the Cross. When His members are tempted to say: It is too much that I am asked to do, they can and should recall how far He went. Through Him, through consideration of His generosity, they gradually learn to really offer themselves. The same thought applies in regard to Mary: her offering in the original sacrifice was no less than having to consent to the terrible death of the Son whom she loved with a love that was and is literally beyond human comprehension. [9] We are not asked to go nearly as far as she was. But we should be ashamed to balk at things so much less.

We can recall too that "offering oneself" does not consist in holding a procession or in saying: "Lord, Lord, we offer Thee!" It consists rather in imitation of the offering of

Mary and her Son. That offering was no mere ceremonial gesture, it was most real, most vital, most costly. It was simply a conformity to the will of the Father, and obedience, carried out at tremendous cost. That is what it means to offer oneself.

The offering of the Mass can be considered as a renewal of our baptismal consecration. By Baptism, says St. Paul, we were *sealed*. [10] The image was that of the ancient system of marking things as one's own property by putting a seal on the property. Baptism is the seal that marks us as God's property. St. Paul expressed it aptly: [11] "You do not belong to yourselves, for you were bought at a price," the price of the Redemption. Mary, as we saw, shared in paying that price of Redemption. Therefore, as Pope Pius XII put it, she can claim Queenly dominion [12] "by right of conquest". He was using the familiar metaphor in which the Redemption is compared to reconquering the human race from the domain of Satan. Mary shared with her Son in that conquest. So we, in the words of St. Paul, do not belong to ourselves. We belong to our heavenly King and Queen. In the Mass we join with them in placing ourselves at the disposal of the Father, just as He and she by obeying the will of the Father, paid the price of Redemption.

So, in this light, our joining in the Mass with Mary is really a form of renewal of consecration to her.

The Eucharist is both sacrifice and sacrament. We do well to be specially united with her in the sacramental aspect too. We refer not only to the fact that she is the Mother from whom He received the Body and Blood we receive in the Eucharist, and to the fact that she shared with Him in earning every grace, even the graces we receive through the sacraments, but there is also another most important consideration.

We know that although the sacraments do produce

145

grace by their own power, [13] yet that grace is in proportion to our dispositions. We have all seen persons who have for many years received Holy Communion daily, but who yet show little if any signs of spiritual growth. Of course, we must be careful not to judge others, and we know that it is difficult to know the inner heart of any other man. Further, small faults, especially those that come from indeliberate actions, things in which a person is caught off guard, do not prove anything much about the spiritual state of the soul in whom they are found. Yet we can say for sure that it is at least theoretically possible for a person to receive Holy Communion daily for years and to make scant progress, simply because he or she does not make the best use of the sacrament. In fact, it could happen that a person might grow too familiar, too accustomed to this great sacrament, and by that very fact, almost become unreceptive, unmoved. We are not, of course, speaking of mere emotion. As we saw in chapter 14, feelings are not the measure of religious response.

Pope John in the passage we considered at the start of this chapter spoke of her as "the most perfect model of union with Jesus our Head". Obviously, we do well to imitate her union at the time of Communion, and also to ask her help. She was the one who first welcomed Him on this earth. He had chosen for Himself all the worst conditions of His birth: the stable, cold, poverty, persecution by Herod. But He found in the warmth of her love an ample counter-balance. If we ask her to be with us during those precious moments, we will have a better welcome for Him. We can ask her to take our imperfect dispositions, to refine them, to join to our poor love the immense love of her Immaculate Heart.

This we can do not only during the rather brief period of thanksgiving that is now built into the Mass. It is entirely

146

proper to prolong that time by staying a bit after the ceremonial dismissal. The public prayers have ended but there is no inconsistency in continuing our personal union with her Son, still present within us. In being united to Him, we are by that very fact united to her, for they are inseparable. [14]

NOTES

1. See AAS 51 (1959) 714.

2. Cf. Chapters 2-3 above.

3. On the Liturgy § 10.

4. Cf. Denzinger-Schönmetzer, **Enchiridion** 1743 (DB 940).

5. Cf. G. Lercaro, "La Missione della Vergine nell'Economia Eucaristica" p. 50 in: **Alma Socia Christi** VI, 1 (Academia Mariana, Rome, 1952) 38-56, esp. 46-52 and J.M. Alonso, "De B. M. Virginis actuali mediatione in Eucharistia" in: **Ephemerides Mariologicae** II (1952) pp. 202-03.

6. The original Italian text for "in the offering" is: "nell'offerta". Could be translated also: "in her offering". Unless we suppose Pope John meant only a very loose sense of union, we probably should understand his statement as referring to a **present** cooperation on her part.

7. Speculatively, we would say that inasmuch as death makes permanent one's attitude to God, the dispositions of Christ on the altar are not merely a renewal or repeat of those He had at His death, but are strictly the prolongation, the continuation of the very same act.

8. St. Augustine, **City of God** 10, 20.

9. Cf. Chap. 12 above.

10. Cf. 2 Cor. 1,22 and Eph. 1, 3; 4,30.

11. 1 Cor. 6,19-20.

12. Cf. note 17 in Chap. 5 above.

13. The theological term is **ex opere operato.** Cf. Council of Trent, Canon 6 on the sacraments, in Denzinger-Schönmetzer, **Enchiridion** 1606 (DB 849).

14. Cf. Chap. 6 above.

Vatican II stresses the special relation of Mary to the Holy Spirit: [1] "... before the day of Pentecost, we see the Apostles 'persevering with one heart in prayer with the women and with Mary the Mother of Jesus and His brothers,' and Mary too with her prayers imploring the gift of the Spirit, who already at the Annunciation had overshadowed her." And, as we have seen, the Council urges all priests to imitate her in following the Spirit: [2] "They will always find a marvelous model of such docility [to the Holy Spirit] in the Blessed Virgin Mary, who, led by the Holy Spirit, devoted herself totally to the mystery of the Redemption of men."

It is this perfect docility to the Holy Spirit that alone can explain the otherwise inexplicable reactions of Mary after the Annunciation. First of all, one might have thought she would reason somewhat this way: "An angel has just told me I am to be the mother of the long-awaited Messiah. Surely, the People of God ought to have a right to know about this, to share in the joy. And especially, as a matter of respect to the High Priest, I should go to him at once." Yet we know the truth: she kept silent, did not tell the priests, she told no one. In fact, she did not even tell St. Joseph. Again, we might reasonably have expected her to say to herself: "Even if I tell no one else, at least Joseph has a right to know. He is my husband. If I do not tell him, I will be failing in love, for I will put him into a most uncomfortable position. How could he help thinking me guilty of adultery? He will feel obliged, being a just man, to put me away as a sinful woman. And that, to say the least, would be disrespectful to the child conceived within me." Yet, it was necessary to send an angel from Heaven to inform Joseph at the very last moment, when he was on the point of divorcing her. Mary would say nothing.

How could she act in such a way? St. Paul gives us the key. In his first letter to the Corinthians, Paul draws a contrast between the "natural man" and the "spiritual man". He writes: [3] "The merely natural man does not take in [understand] the things of the Spirit of God, for they are foolishness to him, and he cannot know them, for they are examined [understood, appreciated] in a spiritual way. The spiritual man examines everything, but he himself is examined [understood] by no one."

In other words, there are two kinds of men, and two ways of acting. The merely natural man does not go beyond human reasonings, the sort of reasonings we suggested above. Now of course, human reason is good. Paul is not preaching irrationality, things contrary to reason. No, but he tells us that the second kind of man, the spiritual man, is enabled to go to heights to which mere human reason could never lead him. Human reason cannot penetrate as far as the Spirit does. That is why Paul a bit earlier had represented God as saying: [4] "I will destroy the wisdom of the wise." That is, God will show that human reason, in comparison to divine wisdom, seems to be no wisdom at all.

In speaking of the spiritual man, Paul makes a comparison. Just as only the soul within each man can know his innermost depths, similarly, only the Spirit of God can know the depths of God: [5] "For no one knows the things of man except the soul of man, which is in him. So too, no one knows the things of God except the Spirit of God." The spiritual man, having the Spirit of God, is enabled to know the wisdom of God.

Mary had that Spirit, was more docile to the Spirit than any other mere human being. The wisdom of the natural man would have led her to tell everyone of her great privilege. But the Spirit judged it better for her to imitate the lowliness of Him who [6] emptied Himself, taking on the form of a slave ... [and] lowered himself, being made obedient even to death, death on a cross."

Actually, there are as it were three kinds of guides a person may follow in making his decisions.

First, one may do what he wants, when he wants, as he wants, because he happens to feel like doing so. This is really the level on which animals live. It is the level of whim, of feeling. A dog is completely predictable. If he is hungry and has food, he will surely eat; if he is tired, and has the opportunity, he will without doubt sleep; if he happens to feel like anything else, and has the chance, he will most surely take it. It would be merest foolishness to put a plate of juicy hamburger under a dog's nose and say: "Nice doggie, don't touch. Wait till meal time."

Some persons live on this dog level, as we said. And, what is more regrettable, even astounding, many today are saying that that is the freedom of the sons of God, the highest level on which to live. They scorn obedience, say it takes away much, if not all, of the spiritual value of what one could do. They must simply do as they want, when they want, because they happen to feel that way. That was not Mary's way.

Those who follow human reason live on the second level. It is obviously higher than the animal level. This human reason is often aided by the Holy Spirit in a certain sense. But not in the same way as that which St. Paul described as the way of the spiritual man. For the natural man, working by reason, even with some help from the light of grace, still cannot attain the higher reaches of the

Spirit and divine wisdom, for he still basically depends on reason, even though that reason has a certain aid from grace. Reason has to move in a plodding way, from one step to another, in reaching its conclusions. It cannot soar, free from the need of the intervening steps.

But when a soul is sufficiently receptive and docile, then the Spirit will as it were take over, by what are commonly called the Gifts of the Holy Spirit. These Gifts produce many marvelous fruits. They not only guide us to the highest realms, they also bring courage that is more than human, they bring infused contemplation. [7]

But we are concerned here with their effect in guiding souls. Under the inspiration of the Spirit received through the Gifts, a person does not need to reason step by step to the right decision. Rather, the Spirit puts into his mind at once, ready made, the answer that God wants the person to find.

Both experience and theology show a remarkable fact: sometimes this guidance through the Gifts of the Spirit brings *certitude*, sometimes it does not. In general, when the decision is of any consequence, and there is opportunity for consultation, the Spirit does not give certitude. He wants us to refer the matter to the competent authority, if an authority is involved in the matter, or, if not, to consult a good spiritual director. The reason is this: the Spirit loves obedience and humility. [8] He wants us to obey. Further, there is great danger of self-deception in this type of guidance, precisely because the control of careful reasoning is not present, the answer is, as it were, handed to us ready made. Many persons could claim a sort of direct line to Heaven, and, on that pretext, flout all authority. Or at least, they could be the prey to autosuggestion. To guard against such things, the Spirit commonly gives certitude only in those cases when there is no opportunity for consultation, and where the matter in question does not really fall under the domain of any existing authority. [9] The Spirit did not lead Mary to consult the authorities because on the one hand, their permission was not required for the Incarnation, on the other hand, they were too hardened to recognize the movements of the Spirit.

Why do not we meet with more of the effects of the Gifts in our own lives? It is not that the Spirit is sparing with his guidance. Rather, the trouble lies in ourselves. We are not sufficiently attuned to His guidance. In chapter 11 we explained that the attractions of creatures on us are like a gravitational force, tending to pull our thoughts, our wills, our sensory nature to their own level. To the extent that they do that, they make it that much less easy for us to rise to the divine level. In other words, if the Spirit wishes to send me a light, it will tend to move me away from creatures; but if I allow myself to be ruled by strong pulls from creatures, His action on me may not register at all. If I am accustomed to following whim, to doing what I want, when I want, as I want, because I happen to want it—that is the very opposite of the condition needed to be sensitive to His promptings.

To acquire receptivity to the Spirit, we need to follow the same path Mary followed, the way of mortifying the attractions of creatures, of giving up desires for them, of aligning our wills instead with the will of God, the way of preferring humility and non-recognition. Her way is the real way of becoming perfectly docile to the Spirit.

At very least, if we cannot always rise to the highest level—and really, long persevering effort is needed to gain the receptivity for living habitually on that level—we can at least avoid living on the animal level of whim. A great help for that is simply this: with the aid, if possible, of a good director, we form for ourselves a set of spiritual policies. We steer our path according to these policies. Of course, such policies should be revised periodically, to adjust to changed conditions outside us, and to our spiritual development. Such revision, again, is best done with the help of a prudent director. By such a means, if we fall short of the highest level, we will at least avoid the lowest. We can imitate Mary at least at a distance.

NOTES

1. On the Church § 59.
2. On Priests § 18.
3. 1 Cor. 2,13-14.
4. 1 Cor. 1,19.
5. 1 Cor. 2,11.
6. Phil. 2,7-8.
7. Cf. Chap. 17 above.

8. Cf. Chap. 9 above. St. Paul, though Christ spoke directly to him on the road to Damascus, still needed to consult a human guide in Damascus, by divine arrangement.

9. Cf. remarks on guidance in Chap. 9 above.

21 — VISIONS AND REVELATIONS

"The Christian dispensation, since it is the new and definitive covenant, will never pass away, and now no new public revelation is to be expected before the glorious manifestation of our Lord Jesus Christ." [1] Vatican II made this statement in its Constitution on Divine Revelation. We notice the Council said that we will have no new *public* revelation before the glorious return of Christ at the end of time. In using the word *public,* the Council referred to a familiar distinction in theology. Public revelation is that which was brought to men in the Old Testament times, and by Christ Himself. It is the final stage of God's dealings with men, in the sense that there is to be nothing that will replace Christianity. Public revelation for centuries was incomplete. But now that the New Testament has been completed and the last Apostle has died, there is to be no new public revelation.

But there can be new *private* revelations. Some of these "private" revelations are actually directed to the whole world, such as those of Lourdes and Fatima. Technically, they are still called "private" to distinguish them from the public revelation we have just described.

There is another kind of private revelation, that is received by an individual in such a way that it is not intended for dissemination in the whole world.

What are we to think of private revelations in general? The question is quite important for more than one reason. First, the great revelations, such as those of Lourdes and

Fatima, are of concern to all men. But also, we need to know what place in the spiritual life of individuals and of the Church private revelations should occupy.

To begin, we recall the distinction we touched on in chapter 14, of the two great categories of graces. The first category includes those graces which *by their very reception make a person holy*. That means, in practice, sanctifying or habitual grace. We add also actual graces, that is, those graces sent us to lead us to do something good. The second category, which is called charismatic graces, is quite different. They do not, by their very reception, make a man holy. [2] Rather, their purpose is some other kind of benefit, chiefly, benefits for the community or the Church.

Charismatic graces could be divided into two groups, those that produce special effects that seem almost miraculous, and those that do not. Among those that do not have such effects, St. Paul mentions [3] the grace of being an apostle, a teacher, or giving moving exhortation to the church. Those that do have striking effects would include speaking in tongues, healing the sick, visions and revelations.

We are concerned now with visions and revelations. As we can see from the division just given, visions and revelations do not belong to the category of graces that make a person holy by their very reception. For that reason, we should prize them much less than the graces that do make a person holy. We recall St. Paul's vehement plea in this connection: [4] "Be eager for the better gifts." He was contrasting the flashy type of charismatic gifts with the graces that directly make a person holy. So we should be careful not to center our lives around visions and revelations.

There are other problems about such matters. First, the difficulty of ever being certain that a vision or revelation is from God. The Church has been commissioned by Christ to be the guardian and interpreter of public revelation. He has promised to protect her teaching in this public sphere. But the case is different with private revelations. There the Church, at most, will do just two things. She can declare that a private revelation contains nothing contrary to public revelation—a merely negative thing, which does not amount to a guarantee that the revelation is positively true. She can also say that a private revelation seems to deserve merely human acceptance. We speak of "*human* acceptance" to distinguish our response from that divine faith which we give to public revelation as proposed to us by the Church. Obviously, such a declaration by the Church does not strictly bind us to believe the revelation, though it would seem a bit rash to deny it in such circumstances.

Conversely, if the Church rejects a private revelation, we are not strictly bound to reject it too. Except of course, if she says it teaches something contrary to the faith, we should certainly reject that teaching. But yet, it is ordinarily precarious or rash to believe an alleged revelation which the Church rejects. And for certain, if the Church orders us not to go to some place of an alleged revelation, we do have the obligation to obey.

Still further, theologians all agree that even if we can prove that a certain series of alleged revelations is true in general, we cannot for that reason be sure that no error has crept in along with the truth. For the seer can misinterpret, can at times be affected by autosuggestion, can even be deceived by the devil.

Finally, even if we could be sure we were avoiding all these dangers, we should still listen to the warning of St. John of the Cross [5] that even genuine visions and revelations may be the occasion of diminishing the vigour of faith. For by faith we accept on the word of God what we have not seen. By a revelation we have as it were tangible

156

proof, so that we *see* rather than *believe*. Hence there is less need for strong faith. This problem of course applies most specially to the visionary himself. It is less a difficulty for those who merely hear of the visions or revelations. Yet all would do well to ponder the words of Christ to St. Thomas the Apostle who insisted on sensory proof: [6] "Blessed are they who have not seen and have believed."

Also, as we have said, even if we gain the best possible certitude that a revelation is genuine, still, because such things are not part of the main line of spiritual growth— for they are not as we said graces that make us holy by their very reception—we should take care not to center our spiritual life around them.

In a few cases persons have fallen into a special trap of the devil as a result of private revelations. They seem to themselves to have received a command in a vision which tells them to disobey the authorities of the Church. They reason: "Surely God Himself or His messenger has a right to counter-mand the human authorities." And of course it seems that God could do so. But He does not will to do so. For that would leave the door open to endless disorder and disobedi-ence if those claiming a special line to Heaven could over-ride any and all orders of the Church. St. Margaret Mary received many revelations from the Sacred Heart. Her revela-tions have enjoyed most special approbation and favour from the Church. Yet on one occasion where her religious Superior ordered her not to do some things Our Lord wanted her to do she consulted Him, and He told her [7] that He not only desired her to do what her Superiors com-manded, but also that she should do nothing of all He ordered without their consent. He said He loves obedience, and without it no one can please Him.

If we recall the central position of obedience in our Redemption, as explained in the first chapters of this book, we will see why He told St. Margaret Mary to obey her Superior. Vatican II summed it up well: [8] "By His obedience He brought about Redemption."

Now that we have warned of the dangers of visions and revelations, it would be wrong to omit presenting the other side of the picture. Briefly, if God Himself, or the Mother of God, see fit to communicate with us, to send us a plea or a warning, it would be most out of place to scorn or ignore it. Of course, as we said, we need to take proper care to distinguish true from false revelations; we need to beware of centering our lives about such matters. But we should also avoid dismissing them as unimportant.

The Church has shown special favour to many Marian revelations. Most prominent of course have been those of Lourdes and Fatima. Pope Pius XII sent a special Legate to Fatima to crown the statue in his own name, on May 13, 1946, and he himself spoke to the assembled crowds over the Vatican Radio. Again, he sent another personal representative for the special Holy Year solemnities held there. Pope John XXIII on one occasion, when he feared Communist gains in an important election in Italy, had the Pilgrim Virgin statue taken around the country by helicopter.

Pope Paul VI has gone farther than either of the previous two Popes. As we saw above, on November 21, 1964, on the floor of the Council, he solemnly repeated the consecration of the world to the Immaculate Heart of Mary. In the same speech he announced that he would send a Legate to give the Golden Rose to the great Shrine of Fatima. But, far more, he himself made a pilgrimage there on May 13, 1967, and, on the same day, issued his Apostolic Exhortation, *Signum Magnum*, urging all to individually consecrate themselves to the Immaculate Heart—a fulfillment of one of the requests made by Mary herself in the original Fatima revelations.

158

With such encouragement by the Church, we need have no fear to work for the fulfillment of the requests made by the Blessed Mother at Fatima: penance and devotion to the Rosary and to her Immaculate Heart. Even without a special private revelation, we know from soundest theology and from the explicit teaching of the Church that these practices are valuable. Penance is not just recommended, but required by the most basic message of the Gospel. It means moral reform, as needed, and then the addition of real mortification. Devotion to Mary is something the Father could have left out of His divine designs. But He did not omit it. Rather, as we have seen, He gave her an all-pervading place in all His dealings with us. Even if one does not wish to follow this to the most complete logical conclusion suggested in chapter 18, at least he should see that if someone were to say, as it were: "God has given her an all-pervading place; but I do not care to pay attention to her at all", such an attitude would be flying in the face of the divine plan. As such, it would be not merely foolish but sinful.

NOTES

1. On Divine Revelation § 4.

2. Cf. Mt. 7,22-23.

3. 1 Cor. 12,28.

4. 1 Cor. 12,31.

5. **Ascent of Mt. Carmel,** 2,11.

6. Jn. 20,29.

7. Cf. **Life of St. Margaret Mary Alacoque, Written by Herself** (tr. Sisters of Visitation, Roselands, Walmer, Kent, Visitation Library, 1930) p. 62.

8. On the Church § 3.

The Second Vatican Council, after giving its splendid proclamation of the doctrinal truths about Mary, and in doing so, taking up more advanced positions than any other Council in the entire history of the Church, drew the practical conclusion: [1] "This most Holy Synod deliberately teaches this Catholic doctrine and it admonishes all the sons of the Church that they should generously cultivate devotion, especially liturgical devotion, towards the Blessed Virgin, and that they should consider of great importance the practices and exercises of piety toward her that were recommended by the Magisterium of the Church over the course of centuries..."

The greatest of these recommended practices is Marian consecration, as we have already seen in chapters 6 and 18. There are many other forms of devotion which the Magisterium of the Church has encouraged. Outstanding among the others are two: the Rosary, and the Scapular of our Lady of Mount Carmel.

The Rosary

Pope Paul VI, in his Rosary Encyclical of September 15, 1966, pointed out that the words we have just quoted from the Council do indeed commend the Rosary: [2] "The Second Vatican Ecumenical Council, not explicitly, but quite clearly none the less, strongly recommended the Rosary to the souls of the sons of the Church in this statement: 'they

should consider of great importance the practices and exercises of piety toward her that were recommended by the Magisterium of the Church over the course of centuries.' "
The list of Popes who have promoted the Rosary is long indeed. It includes all the Popes of recent times, along with many of previous centuries. It includes Pope John XXIII, in whose name so many claim they are authorized to ignore the Rosary. He not only praised it, but said it himself. In his *Journal of a Soul* [3] he tells us that from 1953 until his death, he himself recited all fifteen decades every day, even in the midst of the heavy work of the Papacy.

The Rosary is also related to private revelations. Especially, the apparitions of Lourdes and Fatima urged its recitation. The Fatima prophecies make the Rosary one of the conditions for obtaining the conversion of Russia, and world peace.

According to some accounts, the Rosary itself originated in a private revelation to St. Dominic. Blessed Alan de la Roche, who died in 1475, writes that in the year A.D. 1206, St. Dominic had been working hard for three years against the Albigensian heresy, but with little fruit. He then went to a forest at Prouille, and there, with long prayers and severe penances, begged the help of the Queen of Heaven. On the third day Mary appeared to him, gave him the Rosary, told him to go to Toulouse and preach it to others. St. Dominic did so, and taught the Rosary with great success.

It is difficult to know what to say of this account. For certain, the value of the Rosary does not depend at all upon it: we have the repeated recommendations of the Magisterium of the Church, and the insistence of our Blessed Mother herself in her appearances at Lourdes and Fatima. Many scholars, even Dominicans, [4] are very doubtful about the account of the vision allegedly given to St. Dominic.

There is a long series of Papal statements, which speak of St. Dominic as the *author* of the Rosary. The earliest of these comes from Pope Alexander VI, on June 13, 1495. Similar declarations have come from Popes Leo X, Gregory XIII, Sixtus V, Clement VIII, Alexander VII, Clement IX, Clement X, Innocent XI, Benedict XIII, Benedict XIV, Clement XIV, Pius VII, Pius IX, Leo XIII, Benedict XV, and Pius XI.

Yet, the language of these statements is guarded. They call St. Dominic the "author" of the Rosary. That is not quite the same as declaring that he received it in a private revelation. It need not even mean that he was entirely original in promoting it: there could have been somewhat similar earlier practices which he refined and promoted so successfully that he could be called the author of the Rosary. We should add that the Papal declarations on the relation of the Rosary to St. Dominic are not really *doctrinal* statements. Rather, they deal with a question of *history*. As such, they do not carry the same sort of weight as do doctrinal statements.

It seems likely that a practice of saying many Our Fathers and Hail Marys existed even before the time of St. Dominic, and that counting devices of beads also existed before his time. What is quite probable is this: St. Dominic made it his practice to give long series of sermons on the mysteries of salvation. In between sermons, to implore the aid of heaven, and to provide a break for his hearers, he had them say Our Fathers and Hail Marys. Out of this preaching-praying method our present Rosary developed.

Saying the Rosary is both easy and hard. It is easy enough for the most simple souls. Yet it is difficult for anyone to say it really well. There are two chief problems, which are closely related: distractions, and meditating on the mysteries.

Some find it helpful to read a series of short lines, perhaps lines from Scripture, between each of the Hail Marys. Booklets have been prepared that are quite helpful for this method. Others will make a meditation between each decade: this is probably what St. Dominic himself did. Still others will be able to continue a meditation while saying the Hail Marys, for it is not necessary to think of the sense of each word or phrase as we say the Hail Marys. Really, to do so for fifty of them in a row would be almost unworkable.

The repetition of so many Hail Marys, and the problem of combining a meditation with them leaves the Rosary specially open to distractions. Here we need to recall the principles we saw in chapter 14 about distractions. As long as we keep trying to banish them every time we become aware of their presence, we are praying well. In fact, a prayer said with a persevering determined struggle, but with little success, will be apt to be more pleasing to God than one said with ease and satisfaction to ourselves.

The Brown Scapular

The devotion of the Brown Scapular of Our Lady of Mount Carmel is another important practice implicitly recommended by Vatican II in the statement we saw at the start of this chapter. For a long line of Popes has praised it. Hence its basic value is established even without the need to investigate the historical character of the apparition reported to have been received by St. Simon Stock.

The Brown Scapular is said to have originated in a vision, in A.D. 1251. At that time the Carmelite Order, newly transplanted to England, was meeting many difficulties. St. Simon Stock, the Prior General, begged Mary for help.

An early Carmelite Catalog of the Saints, dating from A.D. 1507, gives us this account: [5] "The ninth was St. Simon of England, the sixth General of the Order. He constantly begged the most glorious Mother of God to fortify the Carmelite order ... with some privilege ... To him did the Blessed Virgin appear with a multitude of angels, holding the Scapular of the Order in her blessed hands, and saying: 'This will be a privilege for you and for all Carmelites, that he who dies in this will not suffer eternal fire,' that is, he who dies in this will be saved."

The historical evidence for this vision is quite good. We can summarize briefly the chief points, under three headings.

First, the Carmelite Catalogs of the Saints. We have six forms of these Catalogs. The earliest copy that carries a date is from A.D. 1426. However, experts in the study of ancient manuscripts estimate that the Paris manuscript, which carries no date, was probably written in the late 1300s. And that is only the date of our copy: the original from which it was made is likely to be older. Now the fact that the Catalog had several different forms by the late 1300s shows it must have had a rather large circulation in that century. That in turn implies that the original is definitely older.

Furthermore, although the Oxford manuscript of the Catalog quotes papal documents from 1317 and 1347, yet the Old Speculum text (the one which we quoted above) does not mention these papal documents. Now it is likely it would mention them, if they had been issued before it, the Old Speculum text, was composed. Hence, the Old Speculum text seems to go back to about A.D. 1300. That is rather close to the date of the vision, A.D. 1251, close enough for memories to be fresh, especially when we consider the striking nature of the vision.

The second piece of evidence is this: About A.D. 1291 William of Sanvico, a Carmelite in the Holy Land, wrote that when the Order was in difficulties, the Blessed Virgin appeared to the Prior, and told him to go to Pope Innocent. Now the Catalogs of which we have just spoken, do not mention the appeal to Pope Innocent while Sanvico omits details the Catalogs have. The result is this: It seems that the testimony of William of Sanvico is entirely independent of the Catalogs. But the date for William of Sanvico is about A.D. 1291, while the vision should have taken place in A.D. 1251.

Thirdly, we have some supplementary facts which, while not conclusive, are quite impressive. The Bordeaux Constitutions [6] of the Carmelites, dating from A.D. 1294, say it is a grave fault for a monk to sleep without his Scapular. And in A.D. 1287, the Carmelite General Chapter of Montpellier says: [7] "The outer garment, which is commonly called the mantle, is not essential to the Order, nor is it our special habit." That is a quite remarkable statement: the garment referred to had once been considered a distinctive Carmelite tradition. Something unusual would be required to move the Carmelites to discard it in favour of the Scapular. The St. Simon Stock vision could easily account for this change. Otherwise it would be hard to explain.

Furthermore, we have added details on that Chapter of A.D. 1287, which tell us: [8] "They took a white cape as a sign of their religious profession, keeping however, *as before* the Scapular, which was once called the capuche, for the special habit of the Order." We note those words "as before". They imply that for some time before A.D. 1287 the Scapular had been well established. Some time before A.D. 1287 gets us at least very close to A.D. 1251, the date of the vision.

Similarly, we have the minutes of the meetings of a Carmelite Confraternity for laymen in Florence, Italy. Under the date of November 1, 1298, we read that the members were wearing the Scapular: [9] "to render glory to God and to His glorious Mother . . . that she may grant and give us the grace to be able to *persevere in good and to come to a truly good end.*" The words in italics obviously refer to the Scapular promise. And, from the fact that we are dealing with a Confraternity for *laymen,* we see the wide extension of belief in the vision by that date.

However, as we said, the value of the Scapular does not depend solely on the historical character of the apparition. Its general value is assured for us by the fact that it has been recommended by the Magisterium so many times over. And those recommendations, as Vatican II tells us, still hold.

But we can go much farther. Even the very special promise that "he who dies in this will not suffer eternal fire" can be validated by sound theology independently of the historical character of the vision. To understand how this is possible, we must bring into relation two statements of recent Popes. First, Pope Pius XII in a letter to the Major Carmelite Superiors for the 700th anniversary of the apparition to St. Simon Stock said of the Scapular: [10] ". . . may they consider it as a sign of their consecration to the Most Sacred Heart of the Immaculate Virgin." Secondly, Pope Pius XI, nearly thirty years before, had written: [11] ". . . nor would he incur eternal death whom the Most Blessed Virgin assists, especially at his last hour. This opinion of the Doctors of the Church, in harmony with the sentiments of the Christian people, and supported by the experience of all times, depends especially on this reason: the fact that the Sorrowful Virgin shared in the work of the Redemption with Jesus Christ."

The picture is clear. Pope Pius XI tells us that one who is devout to the Blessed Virgin will not incur eternal death. He adds that this is a view supported by the Doctors of the Church, by the belief of the faithful, and by actual experience of all ages. Then Pope Pius XII tells us that the Brown Scapular, properly understood, is really the external sign of a consecration to Mary. Thinking of the words of Pius XI, we might rightly ask just how much devotion to Mary would be required to gain such an assurance. Pius XI does not venture to say. Nor does Pius XII define a precise measure: that really cannot be done. But this much is clear: If someone wears the Scapular as the sign of a real consecration to Mary, one made and lived out in the way we have already described, for certain, that one can count on the Scapular promise. And even if there never was any apparition to St. Simon Stock, still, his hope is founded on the sound theological teaching of the Popes, which we have just presented.

So tremendous a privilege as this should be more than enough to make all eager to take up the Scapular devotion. But there is more to be said. For here is another privilege associated with the Scapular: the Sabbatine Privilege.

This privilege was announced in a Bull [12] of Pope John XXII, dated March 3, 1322. In it the Pope said the Blessed Mother had appeared to him and made this great promise. What did she promise? Unfortunately, the manuscripts we have carry two different readings. One reading promises that those who fulfill certain conditions (which we shall soon enumerate) will be freed from Purgatory on the first Saturday after their death; the other version is less specific, promises merely early release.

The original copy of the Bull of Pope John XXII has been lost. Many documents of that Pope have been lost. However, official transcripts of it allow us to trace it back to an authenticated copy made in 1421. Similar copies of the original Bull were approved by Popes Clement VII, St. Pius V, Gregory XIII, and others as well. If we cannot rely on notarized copies, guaranteed by several Popes, then we had better give up trying to prove almost any historical event. For we do not have notarized documents to support most of the data used in our histories.

What of the variations in the reading? There are two different texts, both coming from the same Pope, Clement VII. In the first one, dated May 15, 1528, we have the stronger reading, promising liberation from Purgatory on the first Saturday; in the second, dated August 12, 1530, we have the weaker reading. The first of these was never solemnly issued, and so is technically invalid. The reason it was not issued may be found in the disturbed state of Rome after the sack of the city in 1527. But, whatever the cause, the copy finally issued was the weaker one.

However, even if only the lesser reading be the true one, it is still a privilege richly worth working for.

The conditions required are not too difficult. Different authors group them in different ways. We can conveniently list them under three headings. First, one must wear the Scapular. Second, he must observe chastity, as it applies to his state in life, married or single. Third, he must recite the Office, the Little Office of the Blessed Virgin, unless, of course, one is already reciting the larger Office of the Breviary. This last condition can be commuted by any priest who has the needed faculty, into something else. Often it is commuted to a daily Rosary. [13]

The second condition, the observance of chastity, does not mean a vow of celibacy or virginity. It means that each person must obey the Sixth and Ninth Commandments as they apply to his current state in life, married or single. What if one sins? It is commonly held that if one regains the state of grace, his claim to this Sabbatine Privilege is reestablished, though repeated failures might mean one would not gain the privilege in its fullest extent.

Are such privileges too great to be believed? By no means, for they come from the immeasurable love of the Mother of all men, who in turn is acting for the Infinite Love that is God, our Father.

NOTES

1. On the Church § 67.

2. Paul VI, **Christi Matri Rosarii,** Sept. 15, 1966: AAS 58, 748.

3. Pope John XXIII, **Journal of A Soul** (McGraw-Hill, New York, 1964) p. 315.

4. E.g., Bede Jarrett, O.P., **Life of St. Dominic** (New York, 1924), pp. 110-12 does not even mention the apparition.

5. Translated from B. Xiberta, O. Carm. **De visione S. Simonis Stock** (Rome, 1950) p. 283. Most of the following data comes from Xiberta's study.

6. Cf. **Analecta Ordinis Carmelitarum** XVIII (1953) p. 140.

7. Cf. Xiberta, pp. 146-47, 243.

8. Xiberta, p. 150.

9. Quoted from **Analecta Ordinis Carmelitarum Discalceatorum** IV, 3 (January-March, 1930), p. 174.

10. AAS 42,391.

11. Feb. 2, 1923: AAS 15,103. Cf. similar statements by Benedict XV (AAS 10,182) and Pius XII (AAS 39,584).

12. Cf. Eugenius a S. Joseph, "Dissertatio Historica de Sacro Scapulari Carmelitico" in: **Analecta Ordinis Carmelitarum Discalceatorum** IV, 3 (January-March, 1930) p. 182.

13. For those unable to read, the third condition is the observance of the fasts of the Church, plus abstinence on Wednesdays and Saturdays.

Vatican II so strongly advanced Marian doctrine and supported Marian devotion that it deserves to be called the Marian Council, yet many have asserted it called for downgrading Mary. Similarly, a great falling off in devotion to the Sacred Heart of Jesus has followed the Council, yet, Pope Paul VI wrote: [1] "This, therefore, seems to us to be the most suitable ideal: that devotion to the Sacred Heart which, we say it sadly, has declined somewhat in some, now reflourish daily more and more, and be esteemed by all as an excellent and acceptable form of true piety, which, in our times, especially because of the norms laid down in the Second Vatican Council, is strongly called for toward Christ Jesus, the king and center of all hearts who is the head of His Body, the Church . . ."

And it is strange indeed, that in an age when there is so much talk of love, there is so little understanding of it. Especially, men think it proper to ignore that aspect of our religion which is precisely the paying of honour to the love of God, under the image of the Sacred Heart of Christ.

Really, devotion to the Sacred Heart is not just a sideline feature in our religion: it is part of the very mainline, the center of everything. For it is, as we said, simply the honour paid to the Heart of Christ as the symbol and organ of that divine love to which we owe both our creation and our re-creation in grace by the Redemption. [2]

Devotion to the Sacred Heart and to the Immaculate

Heart have gone down together. Quite naturally, in a way, for they are so closely bound together. Back in the golden era of the Patristic Age, two great Doctors of the Church, St. Gregory Nazianzus and St. Cyril of Alexandria stressed the fact that if one believes that Mary is the Mother of God, he logically must also believe the true doctrine about the two natures, divine and human, united in the one Divine Person of Christ. Actual experience of that age and of later ages, especially that of the so-called Reformation, shows how right these two Doctors were. Those who rejected Mary's divine Motherhood ended by rejecting also the divinity of her Son. Similarly, many today who began by dropping their interest in Mary and in her Immaculate Heart, now no longer accept the divinity or the Sacred Heart of her Son.

Devotion to these two Hearts is strikingly parallel in many ways, especially in structure and in motive.

Pope Pius XI, in his classic Encyclical *Miserentissimus Redemptor,* on the Sacred Heart, tells us there are two chief features involved in devotion to the Sacred Heart, consecration and reparation: [3] "But certainly, among the other things which properly belong to the worship of the Sacred Heart, that consecration stands out and is notable, by which we, recognizing that we have received all that we are and have from the eternal love of God, dedicate ourselves and all that we have to the Divine Heart of Jesus."

In a parallel way, Vatican II and Pope Paul VI, as we have already seen, have urged consecration to the Immaculate Heart of Mary.

Pius XI adds this teaching on reparation to the Sacred Heart: [4] ". . . if the first and chief thing in consecration is the repayment of the love of the creature to the love of the Creator, the second thing at once follows from it, that if that Uncreated Love has been neglected by forgetfulness or violated by offenses, compensation should be made in some way for the injustice that has been inflicted: in common language we call this debt one of reparation..."

At first sight, one might wonder if it is proper to speak of making reparation also to the Immaculate Heart of Mary. Yet, on reflection, we see that it is most obviously due: Is not reparation, that is, some sort of make-up, due when we have offended even the most ordinary person? But our sins have hurt her most gravely: they were the cause of the dreadful passion and death of her Son to which she, out of love for the Father, for Him and for us, lovingly consented, at the cost of such tremendous suffering that, as we saw, [5] it is literally beyond our ability to measure it. Pope Pius XII in his great Encyclical on the Sacred Heart, the *Haurietis aquas,* brought out this fact very well, in the course of a theologically important passage in which he stressed the interconnection of the devotions to the Sacred Heart and the Immaculate Heart: [6] "In order that more abundant benefits may flow upon the Christian family, and, in fact, upon the whole human race from this worship of the most Sacred Heart of Jesus, let the faithful take care that devotion to the Immaculate Heart of the Mother of God also be closely joined to it. For since, by the will of God, the most Blessed Virgin Mary was inseparably joined with Christ in accomplishing the work of human redemption, to such an extent that our salvation came from the love and sufferings of Jesus Christ, intimately joined with the love and sorrows of His Mother, it is altogether fitting that the Christian people, since they have obtained divine life from Christ through Mary, render also to their heavenly Mother similar piety, love, and sentiments of a grateful and atoning heart..."

The thought of the great Pope is splendid. He tells us that precisely since Mary was joined inseparably with her divine Son in the Redemption, in the gaining of divine life for us, so devotion to the two Hearts should be joined together, in such a way that to her too there be offered love, and atonement.

This union of the two Hearts was not only a union in the summit of the Redemption, in Calvary. It was also a constant union of Jesus and Mary in all the mysteries of His life, death and resurrection. It is a union that extends beyond the consummation of time into the endless reaches of eternity. It will never cease. Pope Pius XII summed it up well when he said, in the document in which he defined the Assumption, that she was [7] "always sharing His lot."

Vatican II expressed the same truth much more fully. For, as we saw in chapter 6, it painted for us a picture of magnificent sweep of the entire existence of Jesus and Mary, from the eternal decree for the Incarnation, in which she was designated as the Mother through whom it would take place, through each of the events of His and her life on earth, including especially the great sacrifice, then on to His glorification in the Resurrection and hers in the Assumption, and finally to their unending rule, beginning in time, extending beyond the end of time to the limitless reaches of eternity after the final consummation of all things. The Council stressed repeatedly that the union of Mary with Jesus was evident at each point. We saw that this great theological canvas provides us with a basis for a most full consecration to her, so that just as the Father has given her an all-pervading role in all His dealings with us, we might most logically and properly give her a similarly all-pervading role in all our response to Him.

Rightly, then, since she shares in all else, the devotion to the two Hearts could not be an exception. What the Father has eternally joined, we should not separate. Consecration, reparation, devotion to the Sacred Heart and to the Immaculate Heart should be eternally united.

1. Epist. Apostolica, **Investigabiles Christi,** Feb. 6, 1965: AAS 57, 300.

2. Pius XII, in his Encyclical, **Haurietis aquas,** May 15, 1956, stresses this point, and draws a distinction between the essence of Sacred Heart devotion, i.e., honour paid to the love of God in the Heart of Christ, and the particular means used to express this devotion. The former is essential, the latter are open to variation. Cf. also W. Most, "The Theological Interconnection of Devotion to the Sacred Heart of Jesus and the Immaculate Heart of Mary according to Vatican II" in: **Ephemerides Mariologicae** 21 (1971) 29-39.

3. AAS 20,167-68.

4. AAS 20,169.

5. In Chap. 8, above.

6. AAS 48,352.

7. AAS 42,768.

THE AUTHOR

Fr. William G. Most is a member of the Pontifical International Marian Academy, Rome, Past President of the Mariological Society of America, and an Active Member of the Catholic Biblical Association of America. At present he teaches theology and Classics at Loras College, Dubuque.

His earlier book, **Mary in Our Life,** was translated into five other languages, and won the Marian Library Medal of the University of Dayton for the best Marian book written during the Marian Year of 1954.

The present book begins by laying the doctrinal foundation for devotion to Mary, then presents the way of living out the implications of that doctrine in our lives. In both sections it follows closely the teachings of Vatican II, which are frequently quoted and carefully explained.

Since the book is written in non-technical language, it can easily be understood by the non-theologian. At the same time, it contains some new theological insights that may be of interest to Marian theologians.

Another theological book by Father Most, **New Answers to Old Questions,** published by St. Paul Publications, London (1971) presents completely new ideas on the distribution and workings of grace (while never departing from the teachings of the Church). It has received, in an earlier edition, a dozen reviews in European Journals, mostly favourable, some highly so.